Heroes and Legends

Hercules

BY FRED VAN LENTE

ILLUSTRATED BY ALEXEY APARIN

ROSEN
PUBLISHING

New York

Published in 2015 by The Rosen Publishing Group, Inc.
29 East 21st Street, New York, NY 10010

© 2015 Osprey Publishing Limited
First published in paperback by Osprey Publishing Limited
All rights reserved

First Edition

Library of Congress Cataloging-in-Publication Data

Van Lente, Fred.
Hercules/Fred Van Lente.
     pages cm. — (Heroes and legends)
Originally published: New York: Osprey Publishing, 2013.
Includes bibliographical references and index.
ISBN 978-1-4777-8137-1 (library bound)
1. Hercules (Roman mythology)—Juvenile literature. 2. Heracles (Greek mythology)—Juvenile literature. 3. Mythology, Greek—Juvenile literature. I. Title.
BL820.H5V36 2015
398.20938'02—dc23

2014020513

Manufactured in the United States of America

CONTENTS

Introduction: At the Crossroads

An old fable, largely forgotten today, bears repeating here: A youth walking through a wood finds two roads diverging. Two beautiful maidens stand before him, one on the right fork, the other on the left. In a lovely poem by American classicist Richmond Lattimore the girl on the left beckons him forth, hailing him by his name:

> Hercules. Here your way lies, my way. Here.
> Take my hand, I will show you, but see how temperate, gentle and green
> It goes. So shall your dearest life go with your hand in mine. Never fear,
> I shall not leave you. Between
> Here and your days' end think nothing but cool progress, soft-soled
> Walking, sleep for hours, blithe company, agemates outwrestled, girls – yes,
> creamy legs, blond
> Looks; long nights of shorn white rosefall; for sedate age, goods and gold;
> Green sinews, honors lightly lifted, good memories. Look not beyond.
> This is real.

The girl on the right, no less lovely for being so grim of expression, offers something else entirely: struggle, battle, blistering sun by day and ferocious beasts by night. Hunger, want, thirst, and endless battle under all these conditions, and worse. He will die a horrible death, but live a hundred adventures beforehand. Those who love him will betray him, but he will be loved a thousand times more by countless millions he will never meet.

You don't need to be a mythology expert to know which fork he chose.

I knew almost nothing about Hercules when my editor at Marvel Comics called me in the summer of 2007 to co-write with Greg Pak a series starring that company's version of the most legendary of all legendary heroes. While I was waiting for the first face-to-face meeting to kick off the book, I grabbed a yellowing library-reject copy of Edith Hamilton's ubiquitous *Mythology* paperback off my shelf and began boning up on the character, slightly skeptical that these too-oft-told tales would have anything to bring to a modern reader.

How wrong I was.

Hercules at the Crossroads
(Corbis)

The old myths, like a bad game of telephone, have been retold into amorphous blandness – like Will Rogers' old joke that it's not what you don't know that hurts you, but what you think you know, but don't.

You don't know Hercules. Worse, you think you do, but you're wrong.

What I discovered, and continued to discover throughout what turned out to be an astoundingly successful collaboration between myself and Pak was a complex, tormented, violent, passionate character. He was not good because he was noble, but because when he saw a wrong he acted without thought to right it; but, enslaved by impulse, he committed as many crimes as he rectified.

Ultimately, what Hercules is, is a man: the man, the epitome of all that is right and wrong with that gender, and that is why our paternalistic society has remained obsessed with him for centuries. He is a hero, and a worker, and a breadwinner, and a warrior, and a lover. Also, a wife-beater, a philanderer, a murderer, a drunkard, and a lazy good-for-nothing.

He did not choose just one road, Virtue, and walk down it never to be seen again. He has faced that crossroads and had to make that choice most days of his life. And at times he has chosen wrongly. Many times.

So have we all, and that's why we see ourselves in him.

This is his story.

CLASSICAL SOURCES

Wherever possible I've tried to follow the ancient sources to construct my Hercules narrative. As these sources, written across centuries, often contradict each other, I've synthesized as best I could these oxymoronic elements into a seamless cause-and-effect narrative without sacrificing, I hope, much "accuracy," whatever that means in this context, in terms of the original, accepted legends.

Some of the most moving accounts of Hercules' life are in the dramas of the ancient tragedians. Euripides' *Heracles* served as the basis for my and Greg Pak's modern series of graphic novels, *The Incredible Hercules*. The poet and classicist Anne Carson adapted that play and three others into a wonderful book called *Grief Lessons*; I'm using her translation here. Euripides' earlier play, *The Children of Hercules*, provides great insight into other players in this great drama, his mother, Alcmene, his sidekick and lover Iolaus, and his son Hyllus. Euripides' *Alcestis* tells of Hercules' rescue of the titular queen while performing his Eighth Labor. Sophocles' *The Women of Trachis* is a character study of his doomed wife Deianira.

Any survey of classical poetry involving Hercules should start at Ovid's justly beloved *Metamorphoses* ("Transformations"), a Roman account of the ancient myths written at around the same time as Christ's birth. Here I'm using a very "modern" free verse translation from Charles Boer. *The Shield of Heracles* is a ballad of the battle between the hero and Ares' monstrous son Cycnus by Hesiod. As one might tell from the name, Apollonius Rhodius's *Argonautica* narrates the adventures of Jason and the crew of *Argo*, of which Hercules was a member. Bacchylides' *Ode V* relates the hero's journey into the Underworld.

Bust of Hercules in the Metropolitan Museum of Art in New York. (Si Sheppard)

Other, non-fiction ancient sources include the great travelogue *Description of Greece*, written by Pausanias in the second century CE, which I've used to invoke the landscape of the Mediterranean world as explored by Hercules during his adventures. Diodorus Siculus's *Library of History* helps us understand how ancient peoples tried to separate fact from myth. Apollodorus's *The Library* is an invaluable collection of those myths from the Classical Greeks themselves.

PRINCE OF THEBES

The Family of Hercules

Hera, Queen of Olympus, dreamt of War in Heaven. Her husband and brother, Zeus, wielder of the thunderbolt, had seized power from their forebears, the Titans, the monstrous sons of Mother Earth (Gaea) and Father Sky (Uranus). The more human-looking gods were direct descendants of the youngest Titan, Cronus, who agreed to help his mother slay his father for imprisoning her other children, the Cyclopes, in the subterranean depths of Tartarus. After Cronus castrated Uranus and hurled his manhood into the sea, the dying Sky-Father warned his treacherous son that he, too, would be slain by his own offspring. A panicked Cronus swore to avoid that fate, becoming as ruthless a tyrant as his father. Betraying his mother, he assumed the throne of Heaven and swallowed each of his children as they were born. He missed only wily Zeus, who was spirited away by his mother, Rhea, to be raised in a nearby cave. She tricked Cronus into devouring a rock swaddled in a baby's blanket instead.

Once he reached manhood, Zeus infiltrated Cronus's court as a cup-bearer and slipped him a poison that forced him to vomit up the children he had swallowed: the sea god, Poseidon; dark Hades, soon to be lord of the Underworld; maternal Hestia of the hearth; beautiful, passionate Hera; and indefatigable Demeter of the harvest. Once freed, the gods united to destroy Cronus and his brother and sister Titans.

The two forces waged an unimaginable battle for supremacy across Thessaly, ending only when the triumphant gods hurled the monsters' broken forms into the depths of Tartarus to join the Cyclopes, never to be heard from again. With Father Sky dead, Atlas, the general of the Titans, was forced to keep the heavens aloft on his shoulders. Clever Prometheus, though spared the vengeance of the gods in the initial Titanomachy, would earn Zeus's enmity by sharing the divine secret of fire with primitive man, and so the new King of the Gods chained him to a rock to have his immortal guts forever devoured by an eagle, only for them to grow back to be devoured all over again the next day.

Nevertheless the Titans' cousins, the Giants, remained free and unconquered. The blood from the castrated penis of Uranus had fallen in great drops to the land of Phlegra, setting the plains on fire and birthing these incomprehensibly awful creatures who then scattered across the Mediterranean world. Hera, blessed with the gift of prophecy since she was a girl, saw that the time would come – and soon, in the way the gods

Hercules's mortal family was as great a help as his divine one on his adventures (if not more so); his nephew Iolaus, depicted here on a marble slab dating to the second century BCE, served as his charioteer and shield-bearer. (Getty)

measured it — when the giants would unite in rebellion, storm the gods' home of Mount Olympus, overthrow Zeus just as he overthrew his father Cronus, just as Cronus overthrew his father Uranus. They would then break open the seals to Tartarus to unleash the monstrous Titans on the world of men, who could not comprehend, much less respond to such a cataclysm.

But Hera also saw that the savior of the gods would not be divine, but one born of mortal woman who came wrapped in the skin of a lion.

Zeus and Hera could not agree on who this mortal champion should be, however. The Goddess of Marriage insisted on the son of a nobleman, Eurystheus, heir to the throne of Mycenae. Eurystheus traced his lineage directly back to Zeus's own son Perseus, the first and up until now the greatest of the great Greek heroes, the slayer of Medusa and rescuer of Andromeda, whom he then married.

The princess bore Perseus two sons, Sthenelus, father of Eurystheus, and Electryon. The latter ascended to the throne first, and sired a stunningly beautiful daughter, Alcmene. "Her face and her dark eyes wafted such charm as comes from golden Aphrodite," Hesiod writes of her in *The Shield of Heracles*. "And she so honored her husband in her heart as none of womankind did before her."

That husband's name was Amphitryon, also one of Perseus's descendants, a general and fighter of renowned strength who would have been destined

for great things in Mycenae if it had not been for a tragic accident. Having rescued his father-in-law's cattle from bandits, Amphitryon was returning them to the palace when he threw his club at a straggling steer to nudge it back into the herd; but he missed and struck Electryon instead, killing his father-in-law instantly. Sthenelus inherited the throne and exiled Amphitryon for murder. Taking with him his grieving wife Alcmene, the general fled to the city-state of Thebes, where his maternal uncle Creon ruled. The king pardoned his nephew for what was clearly an unintentional crime.

Zeus watched this pitiful affair unfold from high Olympus and was vexed that a noble warrior like Amphitryon had been brought to disgrace by cruel fate. He did not wish to further reward craven Sthenelus by making his son the gods' champion as Hera intended; preferably, that honor would go to the house of Amphitryon and thereby restore some of its tarnished luster.

And, not coincidentally, the notoriously libidinous King of Heaven had burned with desire for beauteous Alcmene ever since he had laid eyes on her. The pleasures of siring this great hero Zeus coveted for himself alone, just as he had sired Perseus by impregnating Danaë in the form of golden rain.

Now, though, Zeus chose a more conventional method of conception. Alcmene had refused to perform her wifely duties until her husband hunted down and destroyed the Taphian pirates who had killed her brothers. Once the general sallied forth on this campaign, Zeus descended to Greece in Amphitryon's form. Slipping into Alcmene's bed he told her the deed had been done, and the grateful princess welcomed him into her arms. Zeus obligingly brought her to the heights of pleasure that only a man who was more than mortal, with centuries to hone his skill at love, ever could.

The Wrath of Hera

A statue of Hera, queen of the gods and the greatest enemy of Hercules.

Once the Queen of Heaven learned how her husband had thwarted her, she was doubly furious. Not only had he thrown his support behind a rival for her own pick for the gods' champion, he had fathered the bastard himself by violating their wedding vows for the hundredth time.

At first she tried to prevent the child from ever entering the world. Alcmene's pregnancy was bad enough on its own: "Weight stretched my womb so, you knew Jove (Zeus) fathered it!" Ovid has her exclaim in the ninth book of his *Metamorphoses*. "I couldn't bear the pain; even now, talking, cold terror strikes my limbs remembering labor; seven excruciating days and nights ... I struggle, yell, mad, vain insults at ungrateful Jove, want to die, words to move hardest rocks."

Adding insult to injury, Hera commanded Eileithyia, Goddess of Childbirth and Midwifery, to go to Alcmene's home and sit by the family altar, crossing her legs and whispering charms to prevent the infant from emerging – at least until Eurystheus's mother completed the labor she was undergoing at the same time in Argos, so Hera's champion could enjoy firstborn status.

The mothers of Thebes, summoned by Alcmene's blood-curdling cries, came to her bedside to see what they could do to help. A peasant woman named Galanthis divined the goddess's mischief and ran across the house, bursting into the shrine and crying, "Quick, fly and tell your mistress, stranger – the princess Alcmene has borne a beautiful baby boy!"

Eileithyia leapt to her feet, stunned at this impossibility, and, thus distracted, freed the struggling mother from her influence just long enough for Alcmene to give birth and give truth to Galanthis's lie.

Hera was just as merciless to mortals who thwarted her as she was to gods, if not more so. She cursed Galanthis so that the farmwife could give birth only through her lying mouth. Whether or not this discouraged her from having any more children the legends do not say; we can only imagine it didn't make the act any more pleasant.

The Queen of Heaven sent a pair of massive turquoise serpents, whose merest breath was poisonous, to slay the baby in his crib. But the world for the first time saw evidence of its champion's great strength,

IPHICLES

Many traditions, in relating how Hercules came into the world, also mention that after Zeus quit Alcmene's bed in Amphitryon's form, the general himself returned, genuinely successful in his destruction of the Taphian pirates, and wished to be greeted by lovemaking from his wife. Alcmene must have been slightly perplexed, as he told her this as if it was news to her, but being the obedient and dutiful wife that all the myths depict, she made no objection to performing her wifely duties twice in one night.

And so, while Hercules was formed from divine seed and Alcmene's egg, a second boy was conceived that same night: the mortal issue of Amphitryon, whom his parents named Iphicles. Twins with two different fathers are not mythic fantasy; medicine calls this heteropaternal superfecundation (one probably doesn't want to know what the fathers call it). Typically, the siblings that result from dual fertilization are not identical (for obvious reasons), but in this instance, since the shape-shifting Zeus had taken Amphitryon's form, we can theorize that Hercules and Iphicles, in fact, looked exactly alike. One can only hope that Iphicles was not mistaken for his more famous brother too often, particularly by Hercules' many, many enemies among gods and men, as the wholly human son of Alcmene did not have superhuman strength or invulnerability to protect him. (Poor guy doesn't even have his own Wikipedia page.)

The legends don't tell us much of Iphicles' life. He fathered Iolaus, the hero's best-known sidekick and

A rare depiction of Hercules's twin Iphicles -- is he hiding his face in terror or simply asleep? -- menaced along with his brother by Hera's serpents in an illustration from the *Dictionary of Polite Literature*, or, *Fabulous History of the Heathen Gods* from 1804. (Corbis)

sometime lover. He served by his brother's side in his war of vengeance against Elis, dying at the hands of that kingdom's monstrous defenders, the Moliones – twins themselves, as is only appropriate.

Hercules plays for his greatest patron, his half-sister Athena, Goddess of Heroic Endeavor. This is a great improvement over his younger days, when the hero caved in the skull of his music teacher with his lyre for criticizing his technique. (Corbis)

(Opposite) Almost single-handedly, the young Hercules defeated the Minyan army threatening Thebes and slew their king, Erginus, himself.

for even at a few weeks' old he throttled both snakes to death with his tiny hands alone. After this astounding feat, the babe's stunned parents consulted with the blind, gender-shifting seer Tiresias, who told them what the whole world soon knew, that Zeus, not Amphitryon, was the boy's true father. In an attempt to placate the goddess's fury, Alcmene named her son "The Glory of Hera," Heracles, or, as the Romans say, Hercules. But their overtures were in vain. Zeus's wife was bent on the half-god's destruction.

Athena, grey-eyed Goddess of Wisdom, suspected Hera would never stop hounding the boy, and so advised his parents to abandon him on a plain of stones outside the city walls. Athena asked her stepmother, Hera, to take an innocent walk with her in the area. They came across the child, bawling from exposure and hunger. Hera did not recognize the emaciated babe, and Athena urged her to suckle him at her breast. (Athena, the Virgin Goddess, could not be expected to breastfeed an infant herself.)

Hera agreed, but the baby bit down on her nipple with such inhuman force she threw the child away from her. Spray arced from the infant's mouth and imprinted the night sky in what we now call "The Milky Way." But Hercules had ingested enough divine breastmilk that he was granted invulnerability, and Athena's aim was achieved. Hera would have to stop attacking Hercules directly, as he was now protected from tooth and claw and arrow and sword by the elixir from Hera's own bosom.

But if Athena thought she had permanently saved her half-brother from Hera's wrath, she had made a rare miscalculation. Hera saw this only as a temporary setback. She was an ancient goddess, endowed with unfathomable power; she could afford to be patient, and wait for the next, best opportunity to strike.

Martin. Heemskerck invent.

The great statue of Hercules's father, Zeus, at Olympia was one of the seven wonders of the ancient world. (Corbis)

Exile and Triumph

As he grew to adolescence, Hercules evidenced much the same lack of control over his strength as his foster father Amphitryon – with equally tragic results. The young man grew so incensed at his music teacher's criticisms that he struck the man with his lyre and caved in his skull, killing him instantly. King Creon had no choice but to punish the boy and sent him into exile for a year, tending to herds of cattle in distant fields.

In Hercules' absence, darkness fell across Thebes in the form of the armies of Erginus, King of the Minyans, who conquered the city in revenge for the death of his father, accidentally killed by a Theban charioteer at a festival for Poseidon. Erginus extracted an annual tribute of one hundred head of cattle in exchange for not cutting off the ears, nose, and hands of every adult male citizen.

In Classical Drama

As can be seen throughout these pages, Hercules was a popular subject of a variety of ancient (and modern!) art forms. In classical drama his family was the subject of at least three tragedies by the greatest of the classic Athenian playwrights, Euripides (c. 480–406 BCE). In fact his earliest play to have survived is *Alcestis*, about the hero's rescue of the queen of the title from the clutches of Death; it was first presented in 438 BCE.

Euripides returned to the son of Zeus as a subject in 416, when his *Heracles* debuted. The tragedy "retcons" the usual order of mythic events and has the hero return to Thebes at the end of his Twelve Labors, having successfully fetched Cerberus from the underworld and rescued his friend Theseus while beneath the Earth. He returns to discover that Lycus, a king from neighboring Boeotia, has slain his father-in-law Creon and assumed power. Lycus threatens to kill both Hercules' family and his aged father Amphitryon, but the hero slays Lycus instead.

If the play ended there it would not be a tragedy, of course. At the moment of Hercules' triumph over the usurper, the embodiment of insanity, Eris, descends on a mission of madness from Hera, infecting Hercules' mind with the belief that his children are really those of his nemesis, Eurystheus. Ignoring the cries of his father and servants, Hercules snatches his bow and strikes them down with arrows. Once he regains his senses he is horrified by what he has done and contemplates suicide, but his friend Theseus appears and offers him refuge in Athens. He goes, a hollow ruin of his former self, proclaiming:

> "So I, a man utterly wrecked and utterly shamed, shall follow Theseus like a little boat pulled along.
>   Whoever values wealth or strength more than friends is mad."

The Children of Hercules, probably written around 429 BCE, involves another group of Hercules' children, those he had with his last wife, Deianira. Iolaus, Hercules' nephew and companion during his Labors, now an old man, flees with the hero's small children after his death from the wrath of King Eurystheus, who seeks to wipe out the little ones so none grows up to take revenge on him for his treatment of their father. The action of the play revolves around the debate within Athens whether or not to provide refuge to Iolaus and the children of Hercules against the threats of Eurystheus to destroy them.

The city's salvation comes when Hercules' eldest daughter, Macaria, volunteers herself as a sacrifice to the Goddess of the Dead, Persephone, so the Athenians can prevail over the Mycenaean army in battle. Eurystheus is brought to Athens in chains, where, much to the surprise of the citizens and the audience, he turns out to be a highly sympathetic figure, denouncing his patron Hera for misleading him into hounding Hercules:

> "I couldn't help myself when Heaven took a hand," he tells Hercules' mother, Alcmene, "and Hera saddled me with this scourge in the first place. Once I had estranged your son for good and knew the fight was on, I racked my brains to make things hard for him and sat up nights to think of ways to beat and finish off my enemies, and end the fear that never left me day and night.

Euripides often played shamelessly to the local crowd, extolling Athens as a beacon of wisdom and mercy, but in *The Children of Hercules* he appears to indulge in some subtle criticism of his hometown, as Alcmene ignores the pleas of the Chorus and demands that the helpless Eurystheus be executed. Classical historians believe that the playwright meant his audience to see her mercilessness as a tragic mirror held up to the city's decision to have enemy envoys killed at the beginning of the Peloponnesian War, a dishonorable violation of the traditional rules of combat. Euripides was not the only famed ancient dramatist to adopt Hercules as a subject. Sophocles' *The Women of Trachis*, while taking as its subject the death of the great hero, is primarily about his wife and accidental murderess Deianira. Perhaps the playwright of Oedipus deemed Hercules too heroic for tragedy, for he is never on stage in the drama, only referred to by other characters. One of Sophocles' lost plays is *Amphitryon*, presumably about the hero's adoptive father.

Unfortunately, Erginus's men went to collect this tribute first from the herd tended by Hercules. Hearing of the threat to his city, Hercules flew into a rage and lopped off the offending extremities of the Minyan soldiers instead. Erginus demanded that Creon turn over Hercules for final judgment, and the king was in no position to refuse – the Minyans had stolen every weapon from Thebes save those left as tributes for the gods when the horde left the city.

Hercules, however, convinced the young men of Thebes to plunder the temples of swords, bows, and spears and counterattack the Minyans as they arrived to arrest him. Though the elders protested this great blasphemy, it seemed to be the only way to save the city. Hercules led his motley band to a narrow pass within sight of the walls, and ambushed Erginus as he marched his men through it. With his great strength, Hercules hardly needed the help of other soldiers. Upon vanquishing this force and slaying the chieftain himself, unsatisfied with this easily won victory, he led the Thebans in an attack against the Minyans' capital. Hercules battered down the city gates with his bare hands and forced them to pay double tribute to Creon from that point forward.

Within this great victory, however, came tragedy, as Hercules' beloved foster father Amphitryon – the only father he had truly known – died in the course of the fighting. A grateful King Creon assuaged Hercules' grief by giving the hero his own daughter, the beautiful Megara, for a wife, and gave him his father's former role as protector of the city, which he performed admirably for years, siring six handsome sons with Megara along the way.

Divine Madness

In the meantime, Sthenelus, King of Mycenae, had died, and his son Eurystheus had ascended to the throne. His patron, Hera, believed this in itself would secure his position as Olympus's champion; but thanks to Hercules' spectacular defense of the Thebans, the son of Amphitryon became the far more storied of the two.

While Hercules was absent on a mission to help fellow hero Theseus, slayer of the Minotaur and founder of Athens, a nobleman named Lycus, descendant of the same-named former tyrant of Thebes, attacked the city, murdered King Creon, and sentenced the family of his champion to death. Hercules returned in the nick of time to defeat the usurper and his forces and rescue his wife and children, but at that moment Hera saw her opportunity to strike.

She visited the Theban protector with a divine bloodlust that transformed his own children into enemies in his eyes. Over the horrified objections of Megara and his servants, the delusional Hercules killed each of his sons with a bow and arrow and destroyed their bodies in a bonfire. It was not until he had wiped out his own line that Theseus was able to force him back to his senses.

Once he laid eyes on what he had done, Hercules' mind snapped. He fled Thebes, hugging the desolate and lonely parts of the world until he finally journeyed to the Oracle at Delphi to give his life some guidance. Consulting her mists, the seeress proclaimed that the path to atonement wound through

even more supplication and humiliation. He would enslave himself to Hera's champion, Eurystheus, for twelve years, and perform any ten labors that he asked.

Though Hercules' pride was wounded severely by news of this indignity, it seemed to be the only way out of the morass of guilt and shame that poisoned his every waking moment and tormented him in every dream: "What good is mankind?" the classic tragedian Euripides has him say. "It is Hera who rules."

As he passed through the doors of the palace at Argos, capital city of Mycenae, to kneel before a king he despised, he had no way of knowing that Eurystheus would inadvertently hand him his greatest triumphs, and make him more renowned than any hero in history before or since.

Hercules Firing Arrows at His Children by Antonio Canova. (Getty)

In the Night Sky

Hercules, with Hera's involuntary help, created the Milky Way Galaxy – at least according to legend. Modern science has taught us otherwise, but the night sky still teems with references to the ancient hero.

Astronomers have named two unusually large (approximately 330 million lightyears in diameter), connected superclusters of galaxies the Hercules Superclusters. The richest cluster within them is A2151, simply called the Hercules Cluster. Its many large spiral, elliptical, and lenticular (convex) galaxies make it quite photogenic, which its vanity-prone namesake would undoubtedly appreciate. Because of its wide variety of galaxy types, scientists theorize that the Hercules is really several smaller clusters engaged in an eons-long process of merging together.

The Origin of the Milky Way by Tintoretto *c.* 1575. (PD-US)

In the second century the astronomer Ptolemy listed forty-eight constellations, or pictures drawn from creative groupings of stars, visible here on Earth. The fifth largest he identified as Hercules. According to Dionysius of Halicarnassus, the constellation depicts Hercules kneeling in tribute to Zeus, his father, who came to his aid while he battled giants in northern Italy after the completion of his Tenth Labor. The star that forms his head is Ras Algethi, or "head of the kneeling one." His foot rests on the head of the serpent guardian of the Garden of the Hesperides, whom Hercules slew in his Eleventh Labor.

Though it has no first-magnitude stars, the heavenly Hercules contains M13, the brightest globular cluster in

The Great Globular Cluster (M13) is among the most noteworthy components of the Hercules constellation. (PD-US)

the northern hemisphere, as well as a nearly spherical planetary nebula, Abell 39. Astronomers discovered several planets orbiting stars in the Hercules constellation, the most recent in 2010. One star, HD 156668, has an Earth mass planet, which means the author's childhood dreams of encountering an actual race of "Herculoids" like those on the Hanna-Barbera cartoon of the same name may one day finally be realized.

Other constellations have an indirect connection to the great hero. One legend has it that a crab scuttled out of Lake Lerna to assist the hydra in its battle with Hercules during the Second Labor. Hercules paid back the crab for pinching his toes by smashing it flat with his club. But Hera rewarded the brave (one might even say delusional) crustacean with a place in the heavens as Cancer of the Zodiac. The Cretan Bull Hercules captured in his Seventh Labor was said by the Greek mythographer Acusilaus to be the source for the Zodiac constellation Taurus.

Centaurus is another constellation immortalizing one who died at the hands of Hercules, in this case the King of the Centaurs, Chiron, who met his end at the tip of one of the hero's hydra-poisoned arrows during the Fourth Labor. For subsequently giving up his immortality to the Titan, Prometheus, Zeus rewarded Chiron with a place in the heavens. Proxima Centauri, nearest star to our Sun, is Centaurus's best-known element.

EURYSTHEUS AND
THE LABORS

The Nemean Lion

Eurystheus, in close consultation with Hera, chose for Hercules tasks so impossible they would crush his spirit, prolong his enslavement, and, once his suffering finally overtook his ability to feel it, end his life.

The first task seemed utterly impossible all by itself: Eurystheus commanded Hercules to bring him the carcass of the Nemean Lion, a beast known to waylay travelers outside that region of the northeast Peloponnese. He was no ordinary cat, but one of the many detestable offspring of Typhon, most fearsome of Gaea's children. Birthed from vengeful Mother Earth, still grieving the loss of her Titans, and fearsome Tartarus itself, Typhon was the greatest monster ever seen, a hundred leagues' wide in both directions, with innumerable serpents instead of hands and feet and flapping leather bat-wings that blotted out the sun. He vomited boulders and his gaze set all it beheld on fire. He so terrified Olympus when he attacked that Zeus and his coterie fled to Egypt to cower in the form of animals. Only the wicked insults of his brave daughter Athena finally roused the King of Heaven back into battle. He was only able to defeat Typhon by dropping Sicily's Mount Aetna on top of him, transforming it into a fire-belching volcano.

Buried in the depths of his prison, Typhon had little else to do but mate with his loathsome concubine Echidna, the half-viper, flesh-eating "Mother of All Monsters." She was well named; her rancid womb disgorged a line of creatures as varied and terrifying as nightmares to plague the lands of men, among them the man-eating lion of Nemea.

This land lay in a high valley in the foothills of the Arcadians, windswept and damp even in summer. When Hercules passed through her beautiful but desolate vineyards and olive groves and arrived in the village of Cleonae, he found a town depopulated by the monster, save for a lone shepherd named Molorchus, who had the good fortune to be on a far slope tending his flock when the lion attacked.

Hercules took shelter in the man's hovel, and, learning of the hero's quest, Molorchus suggested they sacrifice to Hera to curry her favor. Hercules bristled at the thought of begging his nemesis for help, and knew of its futility in any case. Not far from Cleonae lay a sprawling Temple of Zeus, said to

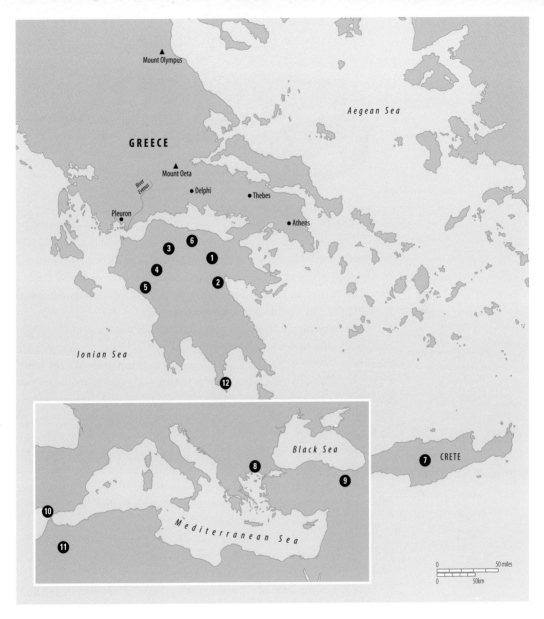

This map shows the locations of the Twelve Labors of Hercules.

(**1**) The Nemean Lion
(**2**) The Lernaean Hydra
(**3**) The Ceryneian Hind
(**4**) The Erymanthian Boar
(**5**) The Augeian Stables
(**6**) The Stymphalian Birds

(**7**) The Cretan Bull
(**8**) The Mares of Diomedes
(**9**) The Girdle of Hippolyta
(**10**) The Cattle of Geryon
(**11**) The Apples of the Hesperides
(**12**) The Hound of Hell

have been founded by Perseus, Hercules' maternal grandfather, which can still be seen today. Should Hercules return in a month's time, he said, Molorchus should sacrifice to his father, King of Olympus; should he not return, he asked Molorchus to sacrifice to his own memory instead.

"From Cleonae to Argos are two roads," writes Pausanias in his second century CE *Description of Greece*; "one is direct and only for active men, the other goes along the pass called 'Pierced,' [and] is narrow like the other, being surrounded by mountains." It was through this pierced mountain pass that Hercules trod, clutching his cloak close about him, as he approached the shallow caves that Molorchus warned were home to the monster.

Fortunate enough to surprise the beast returning with blood-slick jaws from a distant slaughter, Hercules fired a volley of arrows at it; but the shafts bounced harmlessly off the creature's invulnerable pelt. He drew his sword and rushed the great cat, but the blade shattered on its mane. He grabbed a fallen tree branch as big as his own leg and swung it against the lion's snout but it merely exploded into splinters.

The Nemean Lion, belly full of the innocent, gazed at Hercules with the blank lack of interest that is the prerogative of cats, then ambled back into its cave and fell asleep atop a mountain of human bones.

Hercules nearly fell into despair until a burst of inspiration hit him; there was a weapon in his possession against which the lion's unbreakable skin would avail him naught. He pounced on the cat in its boneyard and wrestled it into submission; then, putting its head in a lock, choked the life out of it with his more-than-mortal strength.

He draped the lion's carcass across his shoulders and returned to Cleonae on the thirtieth day after he left, where he found Molorchus poised to make a sacrifice in the memory of a fallen hero. The shepherd was overjoyed to learn that he could make a sacrifice in the presence of a triumphant hero instead. At the nearby Temple of Zeus, Hercules led the Nemeans in rededicating their annual summer games to his father.

Then he returned to Argos, a development Eurystheus did not expect. When his messengers ran to his throne to inform him of his slave's approach, the king was struck with terror. He refused to allow the hero to enter the city gates, but instead peered down from the battlements to verify that Hercules had completed his task. The mere sight of the monstrous lion made him quake with fear. The king demanded that Hercules take it away at once. The hero was somewhat at a loss at what to do with his trophy, but realized that the lion's claws were able to cut through anything – even its own impenetrable fur. So he skinned the cat with its own nails and fashioned a robe and headpiece that would not only afford him protection from all weapons, but remind all who saw him of his victory at his first given task.

The Lernaean Hydra

Fortunately for Eurystheus, Typhon and Echidna bore countless monstrous offspring. Even if one alone could not slay Hercules, surely the accumulation of trials would sap the hero's strength until one of the later creatures could get the better of him in combat.

For years Lake Lerna, five miles from Argos, was celebrated for its cleansing waters and as the spot where Hades absconded with his beloved Persephone into the Underworld. Yet in a cruel joke, into the marshes on the lake's eastern shore slithered the hydra, yet another of Typhon's horrific bastards, to take up residence. In addition to its countless lashing serpents' heads, so many it was said that vase-painters were unable to fit them all on a single amphora, the hydra was so venomous that even its footprints could poison the unwary. So polluted, the waters of Lerna were rendered deadly to all, and the region became as popular as a funeral. The Lernean people were deprived of their livelihoods and the source of life in their wells in a single stroke.

The people complained to the King of Mycenae, and in lieu of an army Eurystheus dispatched his slave Hercules to the lake in the hopes that this second quest would prove to be the last. The hero traveled off in a chariot driven by his nephew, shield-bearer, and lover, Iolaus.

They discovered the hydra's lair in the hollow of a sprawling plane tree at the headwaters of several springs feeding the lake. Upon the advice of his sister Athena, whispered in his ear, Hercules bombarded the gaping maw at the center of the snarled roots with flaming arrows, setting the serpent's home ablaze and forcing it out. Instantly the hydra snaked around his ankles, dropping him to the ground; Hercules crushed as many of its heads as he could but each time he struck off one, two or three more erupted from the stump to hiss and snap at him.

Thinking quickly, Iolaus grabbed one of the flaming branches from the flickering plane tree. As Hercules crushed one head, his young shield-bearer cauterized the wound with the torch, preventing new heads from sprouting. In this manner Hercules and his ward successfully separated all the hydra's countless heads from its countless necks.

Again Hercules returned to Mycenae with his prize, and again Eurystheus was too terrified to allow him entry; in fact, he refused to recognize the Second Labor as completed because it was Iolaus, not Hercules himself, who was the means of the monster's destruction. (Once news of Hercules' success spread, the king's opinion would very much be in the minority in this.) Hercules shrugged and once again claimed the unwanted trophy for himself. Slicing open the serpent's belly and discovering the gall that was the source of the hydra's poison, he dipped his arrowheads in the bile to make their points instantly lethal.

And in doing so, he unwittingly engineered his own destruction.

The Ceryneian Hind

Stymied twice in engineering the death of Hercules by the tooth and claw of monsters, Hera switched tactics and tried to foster bad blood between the hero and her fellow gods. Eurystheus next charged Hercules with the capture of the Ceryneian Hind, sometimes mistakenly called a stag because of her golden horns. But this deer was a female, sacred to that most formidable of goddesses, Artemis, wild maiden of the hunt. As a girl frolicking in the foothills of the Parrhasians, Artemis had caught sight of a herd of five mammoth hinds, and chased them down barefoot. All but one she harnessed to her chariot; the fifth sprang across the River Celadon to freedom. Hera suspected that if Hercules could achieve what Artemis could not, the hero would feel the full force of the huntress's wrath.

Hercules wisely recognized that this challenge was one not of strength, but of endurance, an attribute he also possessed in abundance. Taking up his bow and arrows (not the ones laced with the gall of the hydra), he made his way to the Ceryneian Hill, where he spotted a flash of gold from the hind's antlers through the trees, and found the hulking deer drinking from a dark-pebbled spring.

He fired an arrow at her leg, hoping to slow her down, but the hind sprang away on the creak of the bowstring, able to outrun even the swiftest arrow. Hercules took off in pursuit, and the loping deer led him on a desperate pursuit across Greece, north into warlike Thrace, wading across the Adriatic to the Istria Peninsula, in what is now (mostly) Croatia, and all the way up to "Hyperborea," which Diodorus Siculus, a first-century BCE Greek historian, claimed was how the ancient Greeks referred to Great Britain:

Greek women in traditional dress carry the flame for the 1948 Winter Games from the ruins of Olympia, in Elis. (Corbis)

Red deer stags in Scotland. Though the gender is wrong, the setting is not; ancient scholars believed the "Hyperborea" to which Hercules chased the Ceryneian Hind is today's Great Britain. (Massimo Catarinella)

Of those who have written about the ancient myths, Hecataeus [a fourth-century BCE historian] and certain others say that in the regions beyond the land of the Celts there lies in the ocean an island no smaller than Sicily. This island, the account continues, is situated in the north and is inhabited by the Hyperboreans, who are called by that name because their home is beyond the point whence the north wind (Boreas) blows; and the island is both fertile and productive of every crop, and since it has an unusually temperate climate it produces two harvests each year.

A journey from Greece to Great Britain, on foot, without roads, is both time-consuming and tiring. And the hind led Hercules on a round trip! Back in Greece after a full year of dogged pursuit, the deer collapsed in exhaustion on the slopes of a mountain named after her patroness, Artemisium, where at long last Hercules pierced her legs with an arrow. So precise was his aim that his shaft missed both bone and artery and merely bound her forelegs together.

Hercules slung the hind, red-hot to the touch from her exertions, flanks heaving, over his shoulders, and prepared to return to his master when he found standing in the path before him the goddess Artemis, Potnia Theron,

Sex Symbol

Hercules' stamina was as prodigious in the bedroom as the battlefield, and many of the tales involving his various affairs with both genders would be well suited to late-night TV.

As part of his exile after the murder of his lute teacher, and while hunting the lion of Cithaeron, he found himself spending the night in the home of King Thespius, who had fifty beautiful spinster daughters. Putting Hercules up at his palace every night for fifty nights while he hunted the lion during the day, Thespius sent a different daughter to the confused-but-grateful eighteen-year-old hero's bedroom each evening, thereby giving the king what he wanted: fifty heirs sired by the mighty son of Zeus.

Hercules had so much experience with women it's unsurprising he was as legendary a lover of men as well, if only for variety's sake. Sexual relationships between an older man and a younger teenager were an accepted part of ancient Greek culture, and Hercules was associated with a number of such *eromenoi* during his life. In his native Thebes there was a shrine to Iolaus, his nephew, charioteer, and best-known boyfriend, where male couples pledged vows to each other. (Homosexuality was so accepted in Thebes that the city raised an entire army unit, "The Sacred Band," comprised of 150 pairs of lovers.) Hercules so loved his fellow Argonaut, Hylas, that he abandoned the quest for the Golden Fleece in order to search for the young man when he was kidnapped by nymphs.

Gay, straight, or bisexual, Hercules was legendary in fetish communities as well. Bondage fans and cross-dressers may be directed to the tale of his enslavement to Queen Omphale of Lydia, in what is now eastern Turkey. He was being punished for the murder of a prince and the messenger god Hermes served as his auctioneer in disguise. Omphale bought the son of Zeus for three talents of silver that went to support the dead man's orphans.

The queen initially bought Hercules to add to her male harem, where he spent one to three years (accounts vary) wearing a dress and a turban, sitting at the loom, gossiping with the other Ionian girls. It was Omphale who donned his lion-skin armor and cavorted about her palace with his club, re-enacting his famous Labors. Their gender

In the most famous gender role-swap in ancient myth, the great hero wears women's clothing while his mistress (literally, his owner) Omphale, Queen of Lydia, wears his famous lionskin and wields his club. (Corbis)

swap was so convincing they fooled even the goat-footed god Pan, who snuck into Omphale's bedroll out-of-doors to molest who he thought was the beauteous Queen of Lydia. Instead he found himself groping Hercules, who, unamused by sexual assault, kicked him the length of the nearby grotto. At that moment Pan swore off clothes as inherently deceitful and spread the story of Hercules-in-drag throughout Olympus, no doubt delighting Hera and the hero's many other enemies among the gods.

Hercules performed his duties as stud well, fathering for Omphale three or four princes (accounts also vary), as well as a few on her ladies-in-waiting. But Omphale quickly realized he had other talents to be exploited. He killed a serpent menacing her peasants' crops; he slew a pair of shapeshifting twins who liked to buzz in the form of giant bluebottle flies near his ears when he was sleeping. In gratitude for these feats the queen released him from bondage early and sent him home to his wife, Deianira.

as Homer called her, "Mistress of the Animals." Every beast from tiniest to fiercest awaited her every order and Hercules knew that if she gave the command, he would not leave this forest alive.

He begged her forgiveness, explaining that he did not ill-treat the hind of his own free will, but on the command of Eurystheus. Artemis sympathized with the hero's position but could not allow her sacred animal to remain captive, for of all virtues the huntress valued freedom the most. Hercules offered her a compromise; as soon as he had proven to Eurystheus he had succeeded in his task, he would let the golden-antlered deer go. Artemis was thereby satisfied, and allowed the hero to pass.

For a third time Hercules carried a great beast to the gates of Argos, and for a third time its king refused him entry. This time, however, Hercules protested; though still living, the Ceryneian Hind was a plant-eater from whom Eurystheus had nothing to fear. He would turn his prize over to the king only if the king showed his face and took the deer from him in person.

Persuaded, the King of Mycenae stepped outside the city walls; as he approached, Hercules removed the arrow from the hind's legs, and she promptly bounded off back to her mistress faster than eyes can blink. Hercules exploded with laughter. Eurystheus was beside himself in fury. The king already had a cage set aside for the hind in his royal zoo and Hercules would have to fill that enclosure with something. He insisted the hero capture, alive, an even more dangerous creature, the great boar of Mount Erymanthus.

The Erymanthian Boar

To complete his mission Hercules had to journey through the wild, primitive lands of Arcadia. The travel writer Pausanias would later write:

> On crossing the River Erymanthos at what is called the Ridge of Sauros are the tomb of Sauros and a sanctuary of Heracles, now in ruins. The story is that Sauros used to do mischief to travellers and to dwellers in the neighborhood until he received his punishment at the hands of Heracles. At this ridge which has the same name as the robber, a river, falling into the Alpheios from the south, just opposite the Erymanthos, is the boundary between the land of Pisa and Arcadia; it is called the Diagon.

Beyond the Ridge of Sauros lay a vast oak forest. Here Hercules shared a campfire with an old centaur, Pholus. Among the horse-man's meager possessions was a bottle of wine that was a gift from none other than Dionysus himself. Parched, Hercules badgered the reluctant Pholus to open it, finally grabbing the bottle and uncorking it himself. The smell attracted the other centaurs in a jealous rage, for the wine-god had meant it as a gift for all horse-men on Mount Erymanthos. When they attacked, Hercules bid Pholus to take cover and dropped the first charge with a volley of hydra-tipped arrows.

(Opposite) The Oracle at Delphi told Hercules that to atone for his murder of his sons he would have to indenture himself in servitude to King Eurystheus of Mycenae, chosen champion of his divine nemesis, Hera.

The great Raphael sketches Hercules battling centaurs in 1503. (Corbis)

Chiron, King of the Centaurs, had led the charge; he traced his lineage back to Cronus himself and was immortal like the other gods. When poisoned by the gall of the hydra he did not die, but simply writhed in hideous agony. Hercules, stricken with guilt over what he had done, followed the king as he galloped away in sanity-blasting pain, finally collapsing in a cave, moaning inchoately. Hercules would not discover a way to bring succor to Chiron until he was returning home from his Eleventh Labor. He found Prometheus, the Titan that had been chained to a rock as Zeus's punishment for giving humankind the gift of fire. Hercules remembered Chiron's plight and prayed to his father to allow the centaur to give up his immortality to Prometheus, so that the noble half-man could die a merciful death and the Titan could live on to eternity. Zeus acquiesced, and Chiron perished of his wounds while Hercules killed the eagle pecking out Prometheus's guts then freed him.

But that would not happen for many years hence. Now, Hercules returned to Pholus's encampment only to discover that his friend, while burying the fallen centaurs, had removed a lethal arrow to see how a single shaft could kill one of his kind so easily. The shaft was still slick with blood, however, and slipped through Pholus's fingers; the arrowhead pricked his hoof and he died instantly.

For the first time since the death of his family, Hercules was responsible for a slaughter. He buried all the fallen half-men with a heavy heart. This time there was no Hera to blame for the carnage; it was Hercules' impetuousness and aggression that were the massacre's sole authors. If he learned any lesson that day, however, history would prove he soon forgot it.

The son of Zeus still had a Labor to complete. He located the Erymanthian Boar by the river with which it shared a name. He startled it from a thicket by making a loud racket, and chased it into a snow drift on the mountainside, there tackling it and binding it in chains.

When he arrived at the palace of Eurystheus the king was so terrified by the snorting, raging boar that he hid in quaking terror in a great bronze jar he had had his smiths craft. For embarrassing him so thoroughly and publicly, the ruler of Mycenae cooked up an even more humiliating task for his slave.

Among the Argonauts

While returning to Argos with the bound Erymanthian Boar, Hercules had heard rumors that a man named Jason in the service of Pelias, the Iolcan king, was gathering an expedition of the mightiest heroes in Greece for an impossible voyage to the other end of the world. Jason aimed to recapture the Golden Fleece from Colchis (in what is now Georgia), thereby lifting a curse on the city. Apparently the Labors were not enough for Hercules to test his own mettle. Like the men who became astronauts solely to achieve the unachievable and explore the unexplored, Hercules tabled his service to Eurystheus for a time and joined Jason aboard fifty-oared *Argo*, named after its builder, Argus the Thespian, and adorned by a prow given by Athena herself that could speak the future.

Among these Argonauts numbered such current legends and legends-to-be as silver-tongued Orpheus, swift-footed Atalanta (the only woman in the expedition), the shape-shifting Polyphemus, and many who would prove pivotal in the rest of Hercules' life, including Augeias, Prince of Elis, and Meleager of Calydon.

But the most important of the crewmen for Hercules was young Hylas, whose river-nymph mother had blessed him with exceptional beauty. Some said he was the great hero's son, others that the son of Zeus had killed his father in a fit of rage, and in guilt took the boy on as his ward. Most said they were lovers.

(Overleaf) The kingdom of Pylus, ally to Hercules's enemy Elis, had its own divine allies to defend her when the hero attacked: the death-god Hades, the sea-god Poseidon, the war-god Ares, and Hera, Queen of Heaven. Athena, who supported the hero's war of vengeance against Elis, fought by Hercules's side and together they defeated the other four gods.

A fifth century BCE Italian urn depicts Hercules with his fellow Argonauts. (Getty)

Whatever their relationship, Hercules took personal responsibility for the young man as *Argo* launched from Pagasae. Because of his fame, the other heroes voted for him to serve as ship's captain, but in a rare show of humility he entrusted this office to Jason, who by this time Hercules had learned was the true heir to the usurper Pelias's throne, the quest for the Fleece being an elaborate gambit to reclaim his rightful heritage.

In her long voyage *Argo* would have to stop for resupply many times. First she dropped anchor off the island of Lemnos, notorious for its wild women who had killed off their husbands for complaining about their smell. Realizing too late that their orgy of murder ensured the line of Lemnos would soon die out, the armored women agreed to help the Argonauts only if the crew spent the night with them. Hercules, for some reason, was chosen to stay behind and guard the ship. (A sensitive nose, perhaps?) In a rare show of self-discipline, Hercules finally had to use his great strength to drag the kicking and protesting Argonauts out of the odiferous-yet-somehow-enticing beds of the Lemnian women and back to *Argo*, or they would have never resumed their journey and the Golden Fleece would have remained unfound.

Slipping past the hostile straits of Troy and fighting back a swarm of six-handed giants near Dolionian territory, the Argonauts were blown off course near the Bosporus. They landed in pitch dark on the land of a friend, King Cyzicus, who attacked them by mistake. Many warriors, including Cyzicus himself, were killed before the error was realized, and his queen committed suicide in shame.

After holding funeral games in honor of the dead king, the Argonauts set off once more. Hercules hoped to make up some of their lost time by challenging the crew to a rowing contest. He, Jason, and the brothers known as the Dioscuri, twin sons of Leda the swan, and brothers to Helen of Troy and Clytemnestra, were the contestants. With Orpheus urging the quartet on with a theme from his lyre, the competitors oared their hearts out. Castor and his twin Pollux soon flagged, but Jason and Hercules continued to match each other stroke for stroke, hurtling toward the mouth of the River Chius.

At last, competing with the son of Zeus took its toll on Jason, and he simply collapsed; but before he could let out of a roar of victory, Hercules' oar snapped, disqualifying him. *Argo* beached on the riverbank and Hercules was obliged to search the forest for lumber for a suitable replacement oar.

Hylas came with him to fetch water but the two became separated in the dense wood. The youth bent down to fill his jug from a spring, unaware that it swarmed with nymphs who were bewitched by his beauty. Willing to share him with none, the water-ladies leapt from the spring and pulled him down, down deep, to their underwater grotto, never to be seen again.

Some time later Hercules returned to *Argo* with a tree trunk over one shoulder to make a suitable oar and Polyphemus had to give him the bad news, as reported by Apollonius Rhodius in his *Argonautica*:

> My poor friend, I shall be the first to bring thee tidings of bitter woe. Hylas has gone to the well and has not returned safe, but robbers have attacked and are carrying him off, or beasts are tearing him to pieces; I heard his cry.
>
> Thus he spake; and when Heracles heard his words, sweat in abundance poured down from his temples and the black blood boiled beneath his heart. And in wrath he hurled the pine to the ground and hurried along the path whither his feet bore on his impetuous soul. And as when a bull stung by a gadfly tears along, leaving the meadows and the marsh land, and recks not of herdsmen or herd, but presses on, now without cheek, now standing still, and raising his broad neck he bellows loudly, stung by the maddening fly; so he in his frenzy now would ply his swift knees unresting, now again would cease from toil and shout afar with loud pealing cry.

"Hylas!" That name bellowed from Hercules' throat across the countryside, but the hero found only an urn lying by a lonely spring. Jason could not persuade Hercules to quit the search and, at last, *Argo* was forced to sail off without him. Hercules would never lay eyes on the Golden Fleece, and, having failed to ever find his friend, returned to Argos and his Labors, admitting a rare defeat.

Return to the Labors

The Augeian Stables

Elis was a vast kingdom in the Peloponnesus ruled by Augeias, a man of uncertain lineage. Some said he was the son of Poseidon, which would explain why he enjoyed riches as vast as the sea. By divine favor his livestock were infinitely fertile and immune from disease, so before too long his stables burst with cattle – as well as the dung they left behind. The stables had not been cleared for thirty years, and if its stench wasn't bad enough, the refuse spilled down the hill into the fields below, which could not be tilled when they were ankle-deep with enormous turds.

The situation had gotten so out of hand and Augeias so desperate that when Hercules arrived from Mycenae with orders to clean out the stables, he promised to give the son of Zeus one tenth of his herd if he could complete the task in a single day. Hercules and Augeias had served together on the *Argo*, so the hero took the king at his word.

Thus inspired, he climbed to the valley where the rivers Alpheus and Peneus ran, and with his bare hands punched channels from each bank into a single canal that flowed into a breach he had made in the wall of the stables. The deluge rushed through and carried the mountain of dung to the sea. The flood caused a terrifying commotion, and perhaps a cow or sheep or farmer or child or two were lost as well, but Augeias's stables were dripping clean in a matter of seconds, much less a single day.

Nevertheless, Augeias was furious, his temper no doubt inflamed by the sudden violence with which Hercules completed his task. He refused to uphold his end of the bargain, claiming the credit should go to the rivers and their gods for the task, not Hercules himself. Hercules demanded satisfaction and called on a panel of judges to decide the case, but when Augeias's own son Phyleus took the son of Zeus's side the King of Elis could contain his anger no longer and banished both from his realm, never to return.

To add insult to injury, when Hercules returned to Mycenae he discovered that Eurystheus also refused to count this Labor against his total because he had entered into a side bargain with a third party. There were supposed to be ten Labors, so Hercules should have been halfway done; but since the king only counted three as successfully completed, he still had seven left to go.

A bronze statue of Hercules, from second century Rome. (PD-US)

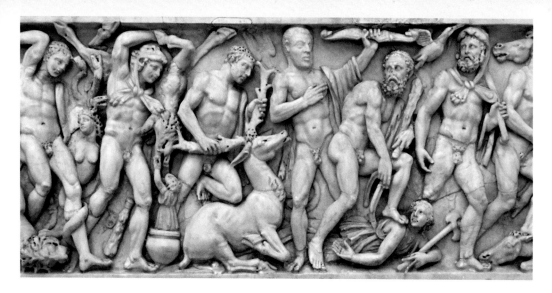

A relief sculpture from the side of a Roman sarcophagus depicting the twelve labors of Hercules. (PD-US)

The Stymphalian Birds

Eurystheus's next task for Hercules cleverly combined two themes of previous Labors into one: placing the hero in jeopardy both from deadly monsters and from the wrath of angry gods.

Incurring the fury of Ares, the feared God of War, was a much surer thing than the king's attempt to anger Artemis. For one thing, as the son of Hera, he had a natural reason to despise his mother's nemesis. For another, he was one of the few gods with competition for his particular sphere of influence. Infrequently worshipped for embodying the blood-caked savagery of battle, Ares was greatly overshadowed by his half-sister Athena, goddess of the more noble aspects of war such as tactics and strategy. Athena loved Hercules as a hero of heroes, so a strike against him would be a strike against Ares' hated rival.

For reasons as hazy as the fog of war, Ares had unleashed upon the world monstrous man-eating birds with armored feathers and bronze beaks. They migrated to Lake Stymphalia, in Arcadia, where they feasted on hapless travelers and befouled the waters with their dung.

Hercules arrived at the marshes on the farthest shore to drive the birds away with his lethal arrows, but there were simply too many of them. The situation seemed helpless until Athena came to his rescue. Relishing the opportunity to thwart her rival, the Goddess of Wisdom gave her half-brother a pair of bronze castanets (some say a rattle). With this he was able to make such a terrible cacophony that even man-eating birds were startled into flight. He killed as many as he could with his bow; the others fled to the Isle of Ares in the Black Sea, where Jason and his Argonauts finished them off.

Nonetheless, one of Eurystheus's aims had been achieved; Ares would nurse a grudge for this insult from Hercules, and would discover the means to avenge himself soon enough.

The Cretan Bull

Hercules would have been well familiar with Crete's history with bulls; it was his dear friend Theseus who had navigated her labyrinth and slain her Minotaur. That monster's sire was an enormous snow-white bull that Poseidon sent to King Minos as a sign of favor for his rule. Minos was supposed to sacrifice the beast to the sea god but the creature's beauty persuaded him to keep it as the primary attraction of his royal menagerie.

The gods do not take kindly to such selfishness. To punish Minos, Aphrodite made his wife, Pasiphaë, fall madly in love with the bull; nine months after this romance was consummated, a baby Minotaur was born. The horrified Minos imprisoned this aberration in a subterranean maze.

But the snow-white bull remained and was driven into a rage by the death of its son at Theseus's hands, rampaging from one end to the other of the island nation, kicking down walls, trampling crops, and goring innocents. It belched fire at anyone who ventured near it and, besides, as it was sacred to Poseidon, killing it in a non-sacrificial fashion would be a grave sin.

Hercules and the Stymphalian Birds by Albrecht Durer, 1600. (Getty)

Minos appealed to his ally Eurystheus. Needing extra Labors anyway, since he refused to count two towards Hercules' total, the King of Mycenae sent his superhuman slave to subdue the raging beast. Fortunately, as bulls were sacred to his father, Zeus, Hercules was skilled at bull-leaping, a sport peculiar to an ancient form of worship, particularly in Crete; athletes leapt over the animal using its horns for a grip, like the handles on a modern gymnastics pommel horse.

Hercules was able to vault onto the bull in this fashion and wrestled it into submission. He dragged it all the way to the gates of Argos, where the usually timorous Eurystheus was inspired to rededicate it to his patroness, Hera. But the Queen of Olympus refused to accept any token of esteem brought to her by hated Hercules, so she freed the bull before it could be sacrificed. The albino brute then terrorized mainland Greece until none other than Theseus himself subdued it for a second time and brought it to Athens, where it was at last sacrificed, now to the city's – and Hercules' – patron goddess, Athena.

The Mares of Diomedes

Thrace, a land below the Balkans in what is now mostly Bulgaria, though bordering also on Greece and Turkey, was oft described by the ancients as "warlike." Indeed, the Greeks said Ares lived there and the whole region was named after the war-god's son, Thrax. The most warlike of the Thracians was a tribe called the Bistones, who lived between the lake of the same name and the Aegean Sea. And the most warlike Bistone was their king, Diomedes – not to be confused with the later hero of the Trojan War – who kept as his personal mounts four raging she-horses fed on human flesh. Eurystheus ordered Hercules to bring him those mares.

Hercules set sail across the Aegean with a few companions and docked along the way to spend the night in the palace of his friend, the former Argonaut, King Admetus of Thessaly. Admetus greeted the hero in a funeral robes and with red eyes; taken aback, Hercules said he could come back at another time, but such was the value placed on hospitality among the Thessalonians that the king would hear none of it.

The Plain of Argos, Mycenae. Eurystheus's guards could see Hercules returning from any of his Twelve Labors from quite a distance atop his palace walls, and warn their master what monsters, living or dead, the son of Zeus carried with him. (Corbis)

An ancient tomb in central Macedonia. Euripides's tragedy *Alcestis* tells the story of Hercules entering the mausoleum of the eponymous queen to wrestle her back from Death. (Getty)

"Who has died?" Hercules asked.

"None of my blood relations," the grieving king said, after a pause.

Admetus installed Hercules in a room far from the dirges and weeping of the funeral itself, and sent servants over with food and drink. Not long after Admetus excused himself to attend the rites, Hercules became good and drunk, singing off-color songs and inviting the slaves to join him.

One of the braver servants chastised him, provoking the son of Zeus's infamous wrath, but before he caved in the offending slave's head with a fist, he demanded to know the name of the recently deceased.

"Queen Alcestis," the man stammered, "King Admetus's wife!"

Hercules sobered instantly, and soon the whole story came out. For his service to the god Apollo, the King of Thessaly had received a rare gift. The Fates were soon to clip his thread of life, but he would be spared if he could find another to take his place. The terrified king went from servant to subject to relation to convince someone to give up their life for his; he

AT THE MOVIES

The best-known cinematic Hercules, Steve Reeves, only played the Greek hero in two Italian movies, *Le fatiche di Ercole* (*Hercules*, 1958) and *Ercole e la regina di Lidia* (*Hercules and the Queen of Lydia*, released in the United States as *Hercules Unchained*, 1959) but, in view of his Montana good looks, action-figure pectoral muscles, and testosterone-fueled emoting, it's not surprising he left such an indelible impression on the role. The movies themselves are lavish productions given their budget constraints, goofy fun mishmashes of the myths themselves – *Hercules* cribs large portions of the Argonauts story, and *Unchained* is a motley Frankenstein of *Seven Against Thebes* by Aeschylus, *Oedipus at Colonus* by Sophocles, and (as its Italian title implies) tales of Hercules' enslavement to Queen Omphale. Though the films catapulted Reeves to European stardom, he didn't want to be stuck in the role, and turned down a part in a Spaghetti Western in order to leave Italy. Clint Eastwood took the part of The Man with No Name in *A Fistful of Dollars* in Reeves's stead, so perhaps he acted a little hastily there.

Reeves had been a bodybuilder since high school, and a beefcake physique was thought de rigueur for the role of Hercules. We have the son of Zeus to thank (or blame) for providing Arnold Schwarzenegger with his first starring role in the low-budget stinker *Hercules in New York* (1969). Just 22 at the time, the future governor of California had not yet gotten his famous Austrian accent under control and all his lines in the film had to be redubbed. (Fittingly, he was credited as "Arnold Strong.")

Although he was the subject of a string of barely watchable grade-Z live-action films, the most commercially successful cinematic Hercules is the Walt Disney Company's animated version in 1997. Unsurprisingly, the family-friendly feature pares away many of the more unsavory aspects of the hero's myths, and as a consequence usual villain Hera is passed over in favor of James Woods's star turn as Hades.

The main thing the cartoon gets right is Hercules' prophesied role as savior during an apocalyptic battle between the gods and their enemies – here the imprisoned Titans rather than the giants. Hades hopes to wrest the throne from Zeus in the coming war, so, in a curious reversal of myth, he administers a potion that turns the baby Hercules – in the Disney film, a god born on Mount Olympus – into a mortal. His imps Pain and Panic abandon Hercules on Earth, where he is brought up by mortal farmers. Disney thus transforms the Hercules myth from Jesus Christ (god born on Earth to save mankind) to Superman (god sent to Earth to save mankind ... complete with cape!). Then, taking a page from *X-Men*, teenage Hercules is persecuted as a freak for his immense strength and has to have a proper modern Hollywood journey of self-discovery before defeating the Lord of the Underworld and his schemes.

As a Disney animated musical *Hercules* isn't terrible, but for someone with any knowledge of the myths behind the hero, it's a curious artifact. (And the songs are pretty weak.) For those craving mythological verisimilitude, however, one need look no further than the greatest in the sword-and-sandal cycle inspired by the success of the Reeves films, *Jason and the Argonauts* (1963). Probably the best movie ever made from the Greek myths, with justly lauded Ray Harryhausen special effects that still hold up today and a great score by legendary film composer Bernard Hermann, Jason has a Hercules played by middle-aged, lithe (but not particularly muscular) South African/British actor Nigel Green. Boastful and arrogant, fun-loving and loyal to the death to his friends, Green's Hercules endangers the crew of Argo when he ignores a warning from the gods and awakens the bronze Titan Telos by looting a temple that the statue guards. Though clever Jason saves the crew, Hercules refuses to rejoin the voyage, and instead remains behind to locate his friend, Hylas. The audience knows, but Hercules does not, that Hylas was killed in the battle, and the last image of the aging hero is Hercules wandering the barren island, calling his dead friend's name. Tragedy mixed with heroism, envy with pity: these are the traits that have defined Hercules from the earliest myths to today.

greatly overestimated his popularity, for he found no takers. Moments from the predestined time, however, his loyal wife volunteered to sacrifice herself. The prophecy was filled, the woman's life-line was snipped, and Admetus was beside himself in grief and guilt.

The son of Zeus was no less ashamed for having behaved so abominably in a house wracked with such keen sorrow. He insisted to his friend that Alcestis was not so long dead that she could not be rescued. Over the protests of his hosts he ventured down into the cemetery and found Death, Thanatos himself, bent over the hapless lady's bier inside her tomb. Hercules assaulted the son of Night and Darkness, lethal twin to Sleep, and wrestled him to the ground until he swore to free Queen Alcestis from his clutches. Thanatos had no choice but to fly away on his raven's wings in defeat. Hercules carried the newly revived woman back to the arms of her grateful husband.

"There is no other story about Hercules which shows so clearly his character as the Greeks saw it," concludes no less than an authority than the beloved classicist Edith Hamilton. "His simplicity and blundering stupidity; his inability not to get roaring drunk in a house where someone was dead; his quick penitence and desire to make amends at no matter what cost; his perfect confidence that not even Death was his match. That is the portrait of Hercules."

Hercules and the Mares of Diomedes, terracotta relief by Johann Gottfried Schadow, ca. 1790. (PD-US)

This epitomizing act of heroism complete, Hercules returned to the task before him. The voyage to Thrace completed, he stole into the Bistones' snow-cloaked encampment in the dark of a moonless night. Diomedes tethered his gore-caked mares to bronze mangers with iron chains, which the hero easily shattered with his great strength. The horses' names were The Fast, The Shining, The Blonde, and The Terrible – though any of the four were apt descriptions – and they rewarded Hercules for their freedom by running away from him at a thunderous gallop that awoke the Bistones from their pallets of fur. Hercules dashed after the mares with the spear-waving hordes of Diomedes giving chase right behind him, bellowing in rage.

Thinking as fast as he could, Hercules punched through the nearest sea wall and flooded the upper part of the peninsula they were on, cutting it off from the mainland and turning it into an island. This accomplished the dual goals of flooding the mares' escape route and diverting them toward the coast. It also prevented his pursuers from having anywhere to go when he attacked them. He then whirled and confronted the trapped Bistones, dispatching many with his club. He knocked the king senseless and dragged Diomedes back to his ship as a hostage. To his horror, he discovered the horses had devoured many of his companions, so to fully glut their bellies he fed them their master as well. Hercules was then able to muzzle the horses, drowsy from their feast, for the voyage back to Argos.

One of the many, many temples dedicated to Hercules around the world: This one is in Amman, Jordan. (Diego Delso)

The Girdle of Hippolyta

The Amazons were among the most feared warriors of the Age of Myth, despite being, or perhaps because they were, an all-female society. Their name means "breastless," and though the story circulated that they had one or both breasts removed to improve their archery skills, all ancient art depicts them with the full complement of two. This would only stand to reason; female archers have drawn back bowstrings for centuries without their bosoms getting in the way.

Maybe the term "breastless" was meant to be metaphorical, for Amazons displayed few of what are traditionally thought of as feminine or maternal virtues. Merciless in war, they held the opposite sex in utter contempt. Whenever they felt the need to increase their number they would raid nearby tribes for men to rape. Once impregnated, the Amazons would murder their involuntary suitors and drown any male newborns that resulted, keeping their single-sex society free of the taint of masculinity. Indeed, Herodotus tells us that the Scythian word for Amazon meant "Killers of Men."

Their queen was Hippolyta, the daughter of Ares and a mortal woman, and the war-god had given his daughter a "girdle" – more like a waist-belt or a sash when compared with our modern versions – to signify her divine lineage and proof of her worthiness to rule. Eurystheus wanted to give the sash as a gift to his own spoiled daughter, Admeta, and bade Hercules to fetch it for him.

Few would have argued that this was the most challenging task yet set before the son of Zeus, and for the most frivolous of reasons.

Hercules assembled a crew of heroes, including his shield-bearer Iolaus and his friend Theseus of Athens. They set sail for the Amazonian capital of Themiscyra at the mouth of the River Thermodon where it flows into the Black Sea, in what is now Turkey. Hippolyta spied Hercules from her palace window when he arrived and was captivated by his unparalleled physique. Anticlimactically, she descended to the harbor where his ship was anchored and willingly gave her girdle to him as a token of her affection.

Hera, watching from high Olympus, would have none of this. To Themiscyra she descended in the form of an Amazonian soldier and raised the alarm that an invading force of men was kidnapping their queen. The warrior women leapt to their mounts and charged the Mycenaean ship. Hercules instantly assumed Hippolyta had betrayed him, and murdered the Amazon queen on the spot. In his *Library of History*, Diodorus Siculus describes the battle that ensued:

Now the general mass of the Amazons were arrayed against the main body of the followers of Heracles, but the most honored of the women were drawn up opposite Heracles himself and put up a stubborn battle. The first, for instance, to join battle with him was Aella, who had been given this name because of her swiftness, but she found her opponent more agile than herself.

The second, Philippis, encountering a mortal blow at the very first conflict, was slain.

Then he joined battle with Prothoê, who, they said, had been victorious seven times over the opponents whom she had challenged to battle.

When she fell, the fourth whom he overcame was known as Eriboea. She had boasted that because of the manly bravery which she displayed in contests of war she had no need of anyone to help her, but she found her claim was false when she encountered her better.

The next, Celaeno, Eurybia, and Phoebê, who were companions of Artemis in the hunt and whose spears found their mark invariably, did not even graze the single target, but in that fight they were one and all cut down as they stood shoulder to shoulder with each other.

After them Deïaneira, Asteria and Marpê, and Tecmessa and Alcippê were overcome. The last-named had taken a vow to remain a maiden, and the vow she kept, but her life she could not preserve. The commander of the Amazons, Melanippê, who was also greatly admired for her manly courage, now lost her supremacy.

And Heracles, after thus killing the most renowned of the Amazons, and forcing the remaining multitude to turn in flight, cut down the greater number of them, so that the race of them was utterly exterminated.

Among the few warrior women that Hercules spared was Antiope, sister to Hippolyta, whom he gave to Theseus as a trophy as they sailed away with the queen's girdle. She would ultimately come to love the hero and bear him a son, Hippolytus. Antiope would be killed tragically by an Amazonian arrow when what remained of her tribe attacked Athens in a misguided attempt to rescue her. Theseus would remarry Phaedra, Princess of Crete, who fell in love with her comely stepson. When Hippolytus rejected her advances, Phaedra told her husband the boy had raped her, and in his fury Theseus cursed his son, who was soon dragged to death by his own horses.

Such was the wheel of tragedy set in motion by Hera's treachery; the extermination of the Amazon race, followed by the bitter end of the house of Theseus. Hera retreated to Olympus to brood on her failures; whether she had any regrets for the deaths she had caused we do not know, for the lives of men are little better than the lives of mayflies in the eyes of the gods.

And Eurystheus's daughter received Hippolyta's girdle as a plaything. We have no record of how long she wore it before she forgot she ever owned it and left it to lie collecting dust in the rear of some infrequently opened drawer.

The Final Labors

The Cattle of Geryon

Eurystheus was growing increasingly desperate. The king had entered double digits of Labors and Hercules showed no sign of losing his spirit or his life.

So the next challenge piled difficulty atop difficulty. The hero would be sent far from Greece, to an island in the Atlantic just off the coast of Iberia called Erytheia, meaning "The Red One." In later days, joined with the mainland, it would become the Phoenician city of Gadir, which would develop into Cadiz, the oldest continuously inhabited city in Spain and all of Western Europe.

Now, however, as Apollodorus writes in his *Library*:

> This island was inhabited by Geryon, son of Chrysaor by Callirrhoe, daughter of Ocean. He had the body of three men grown together and joined in one at the waist, but parted in three from the flanks and thighs. He owned red kine (cattle), of which Eurytion was the herdsman and Orthus, the two-headed hound, begotten by Typhon on Echidna, was the watchdog.

As if a journey to the ends of the earth and a gauntlet of monsters wasn't bad enough, Eurystheus insisted that Hercules bring back the red cattle without asking or paying for them.

Hercules chose to cross the Mediterranean and make his way westward across the Libyan desert, a decision he soon regretted. The blazing sun punished him mercilessly and in frustration he loosed an arrow at it. Helios the sun-god was amused by this act of temerity, and sent to the hero a golden cup the size of a small boat that would take him anywhere he wished.

He floated west until he could advance no further, where a bridge of land connected Africa to Europe. His feet no doubt still covered with blisters and burns from desert sands, he had no desire to disembark, so he smashed his way through the barrier, creating what the ancients called the Pillars of Hercules, and is better known today as the Rock of Gibraltar.

The son of Zeus had no sooner beached Helios's cup on the shores of Erytheia than the hound Orthus bounded toward him, twin jaws snapping and frothing. Hercules crushed both heads with his club then faced Eurytion, not far behind. The herdsman was no match for the hero, and soon the red herd lay unguarded.

Maffei

But Geryon's servants warned him of Hercules' arrival and the giant donned his thrice-breasted armor and rushed into battle. The hero pierced all three of his sides with a single arrow. Again Hera tried to intervene as she had against the Amazons, but in her haste she allowed herself to be visible to Hercules, who lanced her through the right breast with a shaft, forcing her retreat.

Having neither asked nor bargained for his livestock, Hercules began the greatest cattle drive in history. First the red herd thundered across Spain, where, some claim, Hercules left behind followers as colonists. As he herded the cattle from the Iberian Peninsula into Gaul, he fell in love with a Bebrycian princess named Pyrene; their love must have attracted the ire of Hera, for the girl soon gave birth to a serpent, which horrified her so much she ran into the woods and died. Hercules piled rock upon rock to cover her corpse; blinded by grief, he kept adding stone after stone until the piles reached the clouds. These "Pyrenees" separate France from Spain to this day.

Though the northern "Pillar" of Hercules is commonly believed to be the Rock of Gibraltar, scholars have debated the identity of the southern pillar for centuries (probably a mountain in or near Morocco). This rather literal interpretation of the myth in an eighteenth century French print doesn't provide any clues. (Mary Evans)

Next Hercules drove his cattle across Gaul, through land given to Poseidon's giant sons Albion and Dercynus. They coveted his herd and attacked him with armies so numerous that Hercules ran out of arrows defending himself. The ground being too soft to provide stones to hurl at his enemies, Zeus sent down a hail of rocks that his son used to drive back the rustlers. This is the source of "The Stony Plain" (Campus Lapideus) between Marseilles and the mouths of the River Rhône.

The crimson cattle stampeded through the Alps and into Italy. Hercules slew many bandits lurking in the mountain passes, and upon arriving on the Palatine Hill, made the mistake of encamping near the lair of a three-headed giant named Cacus, a herdsman himself. He decorated the entrance to his cave with the bones of his victims and breathed

Hercules Killing Cacus by Hendrick Goltzius. (PD-US)

fire at any mortal who dared come near. Hercules awoke in the morning to discover that the giant had dragged away two of his best bulls and four of his heifers.

He followed the tracks to Cacus's cavern. Smashing aside the rock that barred its entrance, he stepped into triple gouts of flame belched from the giant's mouths. But the hide of the Nemean Lion protected him, and he throttled the giant by his three necks and beat him to death with his club.

On the Palatine Hill he erected an altar to Zeus in honor of his victory; and around that altar would later rise the mighty city of Rome. Further south along his cattle drive the Italian cities of Pompeii and (of course) Herculaneum were said to have been founded by him.

(Opposite) Hercules tricked Atlas to get the golden apples required for his Eleventh Labor. Next he had to trick the Titan to take the heavens back from his shoulders so he could escape.

He waded with his cattle across the water to Sicily, only to discover he had gone the wrong way. He turned the herd around and headed up the east coast of Italy instead. As he crossed to the Peloponnese, Hera again saw a chance to interfere, sending gadflies to stampede the herd away from its master. Hercules had to chase them through Thrace into the Scythian desert before reclaiming most of the cattle. Then he merely had to kill yet another giant, the boulder-hurling Alcyoneus, who stood astride the Corinthian Isthmus, before finally returning triumphant to Argos.

Eight years and one month had passed since he had entered Eurystheus's service.

In Comic Books

The ancient model for the modern superhero, Hercules has enjoyed a life in comic books as varied as his career in myth.

His slaughter of the Amazons was not forgotten by that nation's most famous representative, created in the twentieth century by writer and psychologist William Moulton Marston and illustrator Harry Peters. Wonder Woman is an inversion of the man-hating warriors of misogynist myth. Princess Diana, daughter of Queen Hippolyta, journeys to America as an emissary of a far more spiritually advanced all-female society on Paradise Island to spread a gospel of peace and defeat warmongers wherever she finds them.

Paragon of masculinity Hercules was thus Wonder Woman's diametric opposite, and so it's not surprising he appears as a villain in the character's first appearance in *All Star Comics* No. 8 (December 1941–January 1942). Entrusting to Diana her girdle of strength, Hippolyta gives her daughter her side of the story of the Ninth Labor:

In the days of Ancient Greece, many centuries ago, we Amazons were the foremost nation in the world. In Amazonia, women ruled and all was well. Then one day, Hercules, the strongest man in the world, stung by taunts that he couldn't conquer the Amazon women, selected his strongest and fiercest warriors and landed on our shores. I challenged him to personal combat – because I knew that with my MAGIC GIRDLE (sic), given me by

Aphrodite, Goddess of Love, I could not lose.

And win I did! But Hercules, by deceit and trickery, managed to secure my MAGIC GIRDLE – and soon we were taken into slavery. And Aphrodite, angry at me for having succumbed to the wiles of men, would do naught to help us!

Finally our submission to men became unbearable – we could stand it no longer – and I appealed to the Goddess Aphrodite again. This time not in vain, for she relented and with her help, I secured the MAGIC GIRDLE from Hercules.

Ever since that day the Amazons hid away on Paradise Island from the treachery of the male gender, as represented by the son of Zeus, until Princess Diana decided to leave for the United States and share her anti-Herculean wisdom with the world.

Hercules made sporadic appearances in comics after his role in Wonder Woman's origin, mostly as tie-ins to his various movie and TV appearances. From 1967 to 1969 he starred in a self-titled series set in ancient Greece from schlock-house Charlton Comics (known to most as providing the inspirational heroes for Alan Moore and Dave Gibbons's Watchmen), barely outlasting the Twelve Labors to end at number thirteen.

DC gave Hercules his own, rather bizarre series (with no mention of the indignities he made Wonder Woman's people suffer), *Hercules Unbound*, in 1975. The son of Zeus bursts free of the rock where he's chained in the not-so-near future to find a world ravaged by nuclear war. He rescues a blind diplomat's son and a German Shepherd (yes, really) and battles mutants across a ravaged Europe and North America to uncover the true perpetrator of the apocalyptic conflict: his frequent comic book nemesis Ares, God of War. Despite great art by legends Jose Garcia-Lopez and Wally Wood, *Hercules Unbound* only lasted a year on the stands.

Meanwhile, Stan Lee and Jack Kirby, the primary writer and artist team behind Marvel Comics, had introduced Hercules as a foil for their own god hero, the Norse God of Thunder, Thor, in *Journey into Mystery*. After depicting their ego-fueled clash in mythic times, they brought Hercules into the Norseman's modern-day adventures as a foil when Thor first received his own title. A brash, booze- and girl-loving egomaniac, the oversized personality of the Marvel Herc quickly made him a fan favorite with his guest appearances in Thor and as a member of several incarnations of the Avengers. Marvel's first "mini-series," now a mainstay of the industry, appeared in 1982 and starred Hercules in a far future outer space adventure by writer/artist Bob Layton. An instant hit, *Hercules: Prince of Power* spawned several sequels.

At the end of 2007 for reasons far too nerdy to go into here, the Lion of Olympus took over the Green Goliath's title when *The Incredible Hulk* became *The Incredible Hercules*. My co-writer Greg Pak and I began chronicling the son of Zeus's adventure in the modern-day Marvel Universe, where he was tasked by his ever-exasperated sister Athena with teaching his successor, irascible Korean-American teen genius Amadeus Cho, as the next so-called "Prince of Power." The mismatched buddy adventure comedy shocked everybody (including Greg and me) with its popularity, lasting in various incarnations until 2011.

We provided "sequels" for a lot of myths for modern times, like relocating the entrance of Hades to an Atlantic City casino and depicting Hera as a corrupt corporate kingpin, but some of the most fun we had was in our Amazons story, in which our heroes are pursued by Hippolyta's psychotic daughter, boasting super strength and invulnerability, who hated the male gender and wanted to bring perpetual war to the world. To head off angry letters from DC's lawyers, we named her Artume ... the Etruscan name for the goddess Diana.

Well, since an evil Hercules was a villain in the DC Universe, it made sense that an evil, polar opposite of Wonder Woman should be a villainess in the Marvel U. Playing up the rivalry between the two companies is always fun, and turnabout's fair play in myth and superheroics...

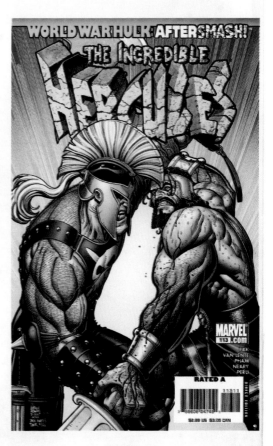

Art Adams depicts Hercules battling Ares, god of war, on the first official cover of his longest-running Marvel Comics series -- itself an homage to the son of Zeus's first appearance on the cover of Thor by the great Jack Kirby – as noted in the lower left-hand corner. (Marvel Comics)

The Apples of the Hesperides

Hercules must have looked exceptionally exhausted upon his return from Erytheia, for Eurystheus turned him right around and sent him back out in the same direction again. This time his destination was even more formidable, the Garden of the Hesperides, on the slopes of Mount Atlas in what is now Morocco. Here grew a tree bearing golden apples, a gift from Mother Earth, Gaea, to Zeus and Hera on their wedding day. The King of Mycenae demanded these apples as his next tribute.

The mountain was named for Atlas, formerly the general of the Titans, who upon failing to conquer Olympus was punished by Zeus by having to hold up the heavens on his shoulders. His daughters, the Hesperides, were entrusted with the care of the golden apple tree, but when Hera caught them eating its fruit she sent a hundred-headed dragon, called Ladon, to wrap himself around its trunk and guard it even from the Titan himself. Atlas took great pride in his daughters' garden, and when Thetis, the Muse of Truth, warned him a son of Zeus would one day strip his tree of its gold, he surrounded the orchard with an impossibly high wall and swore to stomp to death any who dare enter.

No map showed the location of the garden, but Hercules knew that it was where Apollo's sun chariot plunged below the horizon at every day's end, and he still had the sun-cup given to him by Helios. West across the Mediterranean his oversized goblet drifted, reaching at last the grotto of the Titan Nereus, eldest son of Pontus, the Ocean. Hercules pounced on the Old Man of the Sea as he lay sleeping. Surprised, the Titan tried to wriggle away from the hero by abruptly changing his shape from slippery eel to snapping crab to prickly anemone, but Hercules still held him fast. He refused to let the Old Man go until he gave him some insight into how to best Atlas, and Nereus had no choice but to obey.

HERCVLES AND ATLAS

The sun-cup of Helios was drawn to Mount Atlas like a magnet to iron. Following Nereus's advice, Hercules did not plan on stealing the apples himself; rather, he would trick the Titan general into giving them freely. He offered to take Atlas's burden off his shoulders for one hour in exchange for the golden fruit. Showing his desire to be helpful, he killed the dragon wrapped around the apple tree by launching a hydra-laced arrow at it over the wall.

With a mighty groan Atlas transferred the entirety of the heavens onto the great hero's shoulders; even his mighty knees buckled under their incalculable weight. The Titan simply reached over the garden wall and plucked three apples. But the feeling of freedom was too delicious to give up, and he slyly told Hercules he would happily deliver the apples to Eurystheus in person if the son of Zeus would but hold the stars heavenward for a few weeks more.

Hercules knew that Atlas planned to betray him, but showed no sign of it. Rather, he said he would gladly submit to the Titan's request, if he would only take the heavens back just a few moments more so he could rearrange his cloak on his shoulders for better padding.

Artist Antonio Basoli imagines ancient Thebes, Egypt, in an 1838 painting. Hercules gave the city its name after slaying its original namesake, Busiris. Or so the Greeks say. (Corbis)

Atlas agreed, and no sooner had he shouldered the Milky Way again than Hercules grabbed the apples and bounded away down the mountain toward the sun-cup. No doubt Atlas's curses at being tricked echoed across the Mediterranean for weeks thereafter.

Hercules did not return directly to Mycenae, but chose to explore North Africa for a spell. In Libya he encountered King Antaeus, a son of Gaea and Poseidon, who amused himself by challenging strangers to a wrestling match and murdering them when they lost. His temple to the sea-god was constructed from the bones of defeated athletes. Hercules was unamused by the king's bullying and readily agreed to his challenge. After all, the son of Zeus, with the help of his clever friend Theseus, had invented one of the earliest forms of what we call mixed martial arts today: pankration (pan = "all"; kratos = "strength"), combining wrestling with various foot and hand strikes. The heroes used this new art to subdue the Minotaur and the Nemean Lion, respectively.

Both men threw off their tunics and faced each other in the town square. Hercules lathered his body in oil in the Greco-Roman style, and found it curious that Antaeus covered himself in sand instead. This allowed Hercules to grab onto his opponent easily and dash him to the ground.

Hercules and Antaeus cast in solid bronze by an anonymous Italian sculptor from the sixteenth century. Original held in Walters Art Museum in Baltimore, Maryland. (PD-US)

To Hercules' amazement, rather than being harmed when he hit the earth, Antaeus's limbs expanded with increased vigor. He sprang to his feet and rushed the hero, who realized in a flash that the king's mother, Gaea, must be strengthening him as long as he remained in contact with her surface.

Antaeus could not get a decent grip on the oil-slick Hercules; but the son of Zeus easily lifted the son of Gaea off the ground and snapped his spine in half. The tyranny of Antaeus was never heard of again.

In Egypt, he slew Antaeus's brother, Busiris, who sacrificed innocent travelers to Zeus. Hercules renamed the vanquished despot's city Thebes, in honor of his hometown.

The Hound of Hell

The King of Mycenae was at the end of his rope. If Hercules completed one more task, he would be free of the tyrant's power and, perhaps even more ominously, Eurystheus would have failed Hera, and the gods did not take kindly to failure. The son of Zeus had vanquished monster after monster, captured giant beasts alive, slain every mortal who dared face him in combat, and traveled incomprehensible distances.

Truly, then, there was only one more enemy for Hercules to overcome. The one all men want to defeat, but never do. Hades, Lord of the Dead.

This Etruscan vase depicts the bronze jar Eurystheus hid in when Hercules brought live creatures back to Mycenae at his request: first with the Erymanthian Boar, and lastly with Cerberus, shown here. (Getty)

Eurystheus commanded Hercules to descend into the depths of the Underworld and bring back the death-god's guard-dog, three-headed Cerberus, yet another of the outré offspring of Typhon and Echidna. If he did what no man had done before, venture into the Land of the Dead and return to tell the tale, the yoke of Mycenae would be lifted from his neck for all time.

Hercules knew he could not accomplish this formidable feat without help from his friends. He traveled to Athens and sought the advice of Theseus. The city's founder said that no man could enter Tartarus without being purged of sin, and the blood of his own sons still stained Hercules' hands. He had the son of Zeus sacrifice a piglet to Persephone, Hades' queen, and bathe in the Athenian river Ilisos to purify himself for the Eleusinian Mysteries, the fertility and death cult of Athens, centered on Persephone's abduction into the Underworld and her mother Demeter's journey there to rescue her. (Only Athenians could participate in the rituals so Theseus arranged to have Hercules adopted by Pylius, a respected local citizen.)

Charon the boatman disgorges ghosts on the bank of Hades in this detail from Michelangelo's legendary *Last Judgment* in the Sistine Chapel. (Corbis)

Once initiated, Hercules would next have to bring sacred objects to a temple at the base of the Acropolis called the Eleusinion. He joined a procession down the Sacred Way out to the temple complex in the city of Eleusis that gave the ritual its name. Along the parade insults and profanities were joyously hurled at a devotee dressed as an old woman who, the story goes, made Demeter smile at dirty jokes while the goddess scoured Greece for her abducted daughter.

A day of fasting began upon the pilgrims' arrival in the city, to symbolize Demeter's frantic search. Then the doors of the Great Hall, the Telesterion, were opened, and the priests and initiates entered to face the Greater Mysteries. We have only the faintest clues of what those rituals entailed; they were called "mysteries" for a reason, and revealing their secrets was punishable by death. (The great playwright Aeschylus got into trouble for hinting at some of the Mysteries in the text of one of his tragedies; presumably to save his skin the offending passages were expunged.) Of them Pindar wrote,

> Blessed is he who has seen these things
> before he goes beneath the earth;
> for he understands the end of mortal life,
> and the beginning (of a new life) given of God.

The doors of the temple being thrown open represented Demeter's triumphant return with her daughter. An all-day and all-night dance and feast was held in the nearby Rharian Field, where the priests said that the first grain grew. Libations were poured for the cherished dead the following day, and the day after that everyone went home.

Everyone except Hercules, that is, who had a Labor to complete. Soul cleansed of murder and infanticide, he ventured to the southernmost part of Greece, called Laconia, homeland of the Spartans (for whom the word "laconic" was coined). Here at Cape Matapan, the southernmost tip of mainland Greece, a cave maw gaped into the Underworld. It was here that Hercules began his descent.

The sights of the Underworld were not meant for mortal eyes, and were perhaps even more tortuous to one with divine sight; but Athena came down to comfort him when his spirits were lowest. First he encountered the cadaverous boatman, Charon, who ferried recently departed souls across the River Styx. Though Hercules did not have the coin with which to pay him, the hero's mien was so fearsome that the ferryman poled him across free of charge.

Most ghosts fled in terror when Hercules approached; many of them had been dispatched to Tartarus by the son of Zeus in the first place and had no desire for a repeat encounter. Only one shade remained once they scattered, that of the great hero Meleager, suitor of Atalanta, accidentally slain by his own mother in fulfillment of a cruel prophecy.

Meleager and Hercules had been Argonauts together and the son of Zeus was unaware that his friend had passed away. Startled, he drew his bow against the ghost, but the dead hero assured him he need fear no man down here, for they were well beyond the ability to harm him.

He instead asked Hercules for a favor, to rescue his beloved sister Deianira from a life of spinsterhood. As the poet Bacchylides relates in his fifth Ode, he said: "'I left Deianira at home, in the fresh bloom of youth, a stranger still to golden Aphrodite the enchantress.'"

Hercules swore to Meleager that upon his return to the world of the living he would find Deianira and make her his bride, a sincere but fateful promise that would lead the great hero to his doom.

But he knew none of this now, and pressed onward to the gates of the River of Pain, called Acheron, where Cerberus's triple heads rose up with a trio of whines at his approach. The dog lashed out at him with its poison-barbed tail, which the hero's lion pelt deflected easily; and he wrestled the hound to the ground and choked its throats into submission.

He dragged the great dog back to Argos and kicked in the doors to the palace; Eurystheus leapt into his bronze urn and cowered there as Hercules unleashed the Hound of Hell on his throne room. He did not wait for the king's permission to leave his service; he simply strode out of the city, never to return.

He had promises to keep.

(Overleaf) *Hercules Dragging Cerberus from Hell*, attributed to Domenico Pedrini, eighteenth century. (Corbis)

THE LIVING LEGEND

Wars of Vengeance

Hercules had a long list of unfinished business from the Labors, wrongs he was not able or not allowed to right while he remained bonded to Eurystheus.

The first city to tremble with word of his freedom was mighty-walled Troy. During his return voyage from the massacre of the Amazons in the Ninth Labor, Hercules' ship came upon a beautiful girl clad in nothing but jewels chained to a rock in the Hellespont. Hailed from the ship the captive relayed her sorry tale. Her name was Hesione, daughter to King Laomedon of the Trojans. Her woe began when Zeus, seeking to punish the gods Apollo and Poseidon for some slight or another, enslaved them in human form to her father. The two joined forces to build the impregnable walls surrounding his capital. But Laomedon reneged on an offer to further compensate the gods for this task once their slavery was finished, so the furious Apollo afflicted Troy with a plague and Poseidon sent a great sea monster to devour her citizens. The oracle of Zeus advised Laomedon that only if he chained his own flesh-and-blood to the seashore to be devoured by the great serpent would the city be spared.

Hercules would have none of this, and docking at Troy marched to the king's palace to inform him that he would rescue the girl in exchange for the mystic horses that could run on water that his father Zeus had given the king as payment for whisking away the handsome Trojan prince Ganymedes. Laomedon, apparently never having learned the old maxim of under-promising and over-delivering, agreed.

The task was accomplished, though not without difficulty. When Poseidon's sea monster reared its head, Hercules leapt down its throat and spent three days wandering lost through its guts until he found the right internal organs to smash. The serpent's stomach acid burnt off every sliver of hair on Hercules' body but at last he exploded out from the thing's belly triumphant.

Soon he put out to sea again with the two white mares of Zeus – or so he thought. He unwisely waited until his ship was out of sight of land to put the magic horses to the test. Slapping them so they leapt off the boat, Hercules watched in fury as they sank kicking and neighing beneath the waves. Laomedon had cheated him just as he cheated Apollo and Poseidon. Hercules had to return to his master, the King of Mycenae; but he would not forget this slight.

The ruins of Troy, in what is now Turkey. (David Spender)

Now freed of Eurystheus, Hercules gathered an army together to assault the walls of Troy. Craven Laomedon left the citizens to fight off the invaders with torches and farming tools while he fled behind the city's divinely wrought gates and barred them shut. Hercules' lieutenant, Telamon the Argonaut, discovered the one weak point in its defenses and breached the walls. If he thought he would receive accolades from his commanding officer for his initiative he was sorely mistaken, though. Overcome with yet another of his blood-frenzies, jealous Hercules launched himself at his friend, club raised.

The quick-witted Telamon spotted some stray stones from the wall lying on the ground, however, and began collecting them. Puzzled, Hercules stopped his assault and asked his lieutenant what he was doing. "I am building an altar to Hercules the Glorious Victor," Telamon replied, and Hercules forgot all about killing his friend. Instead he vented his wrath on Laomedon, shooting the king down from the walls of his castle along with all but one of his sons. He gave Hesione to Telamon for a bride and said she could take any one captive she wished as a slave. She chose Priam, her one surviving brother, future father of Hector and Paris.

The Trojans rebuilt the wall after Hercules' departure, with one that would not be so easily breached. As Poseidon marvels in the *Iliad*, "The fame of this wall will reach as far as dawn itself, and men will no longer think anything of the one which Phoebus Apollo and myself built with so much labor for Laomedon." Indeed, only clever Odysseus's gambit of a hollow wooden horse enabled Troy's enemies to get past it.

Next on Hercules' personal list of post-Labors labors was the vindication of Prince Phyleus of Elis, who had supported the son of Zeus in court against his father over proper payment for the Fifth Labor. He gathered an army and marched on Elis, but King Augeias was not going down without a fight. The king recruited as his main generals the curious twins known as the Moliones, who were born from a silver egg, conjoined at the waist. Their strength was second only to Hercules' and their martial skill far exceeded his own; the forces of Elis crushed the invaders.

Humiliated, enraged, Hercules vowed revenge, and ambushed the twins from the underbrush as they made their way to Corinth for the Third Isthmian Festival. With their generals slain by the hero's hydra-tipped arrows, Augeias's forces were no match for their enemies' second assault. Hercules killed the king with his own hands and installed his ally Phyleus on the throne.

Having not exactly showered himself in glory in this episode, our unheroic hero salvaged one positive outcome; besides engineering a regime change in the throne room, Hercules also took over Elis's annual festival of sport, held annually at its sanctuary in Olympia. Pausanias tells us that the competitions at Olympia were as old as time, dedicated to Cronus, first of the gods and Zeus's father, by the golden-skinned race of men who predated our own. Looming over the temple complex was one of the Seven Wonders of the Ancient World, the magnificent ivory statue of Zeus in gold raiment hewn by the legendary mason and architect, Phidias. To honor his victory over Augeias, as dishonorable as it was, Hercules declared a new series of challenges to strength and skill, attracting athletes from across Greece to compete in jumping, running, chariot racing, wrestling, and more. Winners were crowned with a garland of olive branches, which grew wild all around Elis.

Hercules won the footrace at this first "modern" Olympic Games, but the star of the chariot races was Pelops, for whom the whole Peloponnese is named. He was in love with the beautiful Hippodamia, but her father had been told by an oracle that he would be killed by his son-in-law, so he challenged all would-be suitors to a race and killed the losers after they crossed the finish line second. From Poseidon, however, Pelops had received a magnificent trap pulled by winged horses. In his haste to best his divine competitor in the first Olympic race, Hippodamia's father's chariot flew apart, and he was dragged to death by his own horses.

Hercules' thirst for revenge was not yet sated. He next turned his crimson-tinged sights on neighboring Pylus, Elis's ally. But the king, Neleus, was a son of Poseidon and a favorite of the gods, and persuaded powerful allies to fight on his side: Ares, God of War, who had never forgiven Hercules for the destruction of the Stymphalian Birds; Hades, whose rage had not cooled from the theft of three-headed Cerberus; the king's divine father, Poseidon, whom Hercules had angered by rescuing the Trojan princess Hesione; and, of course, Hera, who needed no persuasion to destroy the bastard son of Zeus.

Hercules faced these formidable foes lit by the burning buildings of sacked Pylus. First he battered Poseidon back to the sea; the god's trident proved no match for the hero's club. Then he rushed to the aid of Athena, who had chosen to stand by his side on the justice of his claims against Elis. She tangled with Ares, but Hercules' spear broke through the war-god's shield and plunged deep into his thigh; with a bellow of pain and fury the wounded deity was forced to retreat to Olympus. Athena beat back Hades into his grim realm, and Hercules pierced Hera's breast for a second time, with a three-headed arrow.

The destruction of Pylus was thus completed and the king killed, and Hercules installed Neleus's son, his friend and fellow Argonaut, Nestor, on the throne. He would live to be over 110 years old, still around to give sage advice to Achilles and Odysseus during the Trojan War.

The Shirt of Nessus

His promises of revenge now fulfilled, Hercules could now turn to promises made of love, specifically the one to Meleager in the Underworld that he would rescue the fallen hero's sister, Deianira, from spinsterhood.

The princess was far from a damsel in distress, however. She rode a chariot in the army of her father, Oeneus, King of Calydon, and had no desire to give her hand to just anyone. In fact, Oeneus had promised her in marriage to the chief of the river-gods, Achelous, who watched over the largest river in Greece, which Herodotus compared to the Nile.

The shape-shifting Achelous wooed his prospective bride as best he could, arriving in multiple forms symbolizing Earth Mother Gaea. But Deianira was less than impressed. In Sophocles' *Women of Trachis* she laments:

> There is an ancient proverb people tell that none can judge the life of any man for good or bad until that man is dead; but I, for my part, though I am still living, know well that mine is miserable and hard. Even while I was living with my father Oeneus in Pleuron I was plagued by fear of marriage more than any other woman.
>
> My suitor was the river Achelous, who took three forms to ask me of my father: a rambling bull once – then a writhing snake of gleaming colors – then again a man with ox-like face: and from his beard's dark shadows stream upon stream of water tumbled down.
>
> Such was my suitor. As I waited there I prayed my agony might end in death before I ever shared my bed with him.

Hercules Vanquishes Achelous
by Bernard Picart, 1731.
(Corbis)

Fortunately for the princess, not long thereafter Hercules arrived and made his own proposal to Deianira, to which she was much more receptive. But a contract was a contract and Oeneus demanded that hero or river-god win his daughter in battle. Achelous made the mistake of accusing Hercules' mother of adultery for lying with Zeus, and the hero threw him to the ground in a rage. The startled river god transformed into a snake and tried to slither away, but he learned the hard way that Hercules had been throttling serpents since he was an infant. Achelous next switched to his bull form, but Hercules treated him no better than the snow-white brute of Crete, grabbing him by the horns and smashing him into the palace wall, which snapped off his right horn in the process. Humiliated by this injury, Achelous quit the field and left Deianira to marry Hercules the following day.

The Abduction of Deianeira by the Centaur Nessus, by Louis Jean Francois Lagrenee, 1755. (Bridgeman)

Hercules, by this point accustomed to a life of adventure, had no interest in settling down, and instead chose to install his wife in his cousin Ceyx's house at Trachis, north of Delphi. On the journey from Calydon they had to transverse the River Evenus, so engorged by heavy rains that it had broken its banks. A lone centaur named Nessus was offering to ferry travelers from one dry side to the other on his back for a modest fee. This seemed reasonable to Hercules, who paid for Deianira to cross without getting her dress wet.

But Nessus craved the beautiful Deianira for himself. As soon as she was situated on his back the centaur took off in an unrestrained gallop, hoping to ravish her at earliest opportunity.

Not entirely sure what was happening, only knowing that his screaming wife was in the process of being kidnapped, Hercules notched a hydra-tipped arrow and sent it through Nessus's throat as soon as he made it to the opposite bank.

Blood spurted from a ruptured artery and the centaur collapsed to the ground, throwing his involuntary rider. Nessus could feel the poison setting his veins afire but through sheer force of will, he clung to enough life for an attempt at revenge. As Deianira came near he made a great show of contrition, and by way of making amends, he recommended she take his blood-stained shirt off him, for the blood of a centaur was said to be a legendary aphrodisiac. Should Hercules ever stray from their marriage bed, she should put this shirt on him and their love would instantly reignite, as if it were their honeymoon night all over again.

This Deianira did, removing the crimson-soaked shirt and hiding it in her tresses before Hercules found a fording point on the river and rejoined her.

And so the spirit of Nessus left his body knowing he had done some small part to avenge his own death at the hands of the son of Zeus.

Gigantomachy

At last, as Hera had prophesied long before, the giants rose up against Heaven. Apollodorus tells us "these were matchless in the bulk of their bodies and invincible in their might; terrible of aspect did they appear, with long locks drooping from their head and chin, and with the scales of dragons for feet… they darted rocks and burning oaks at the sky."

The missiles crashed against the battlements of Olympus, and Zeus called the gods to arms. He sent Athena to fetch Hercules, the man of mortal woman adorned by lion's skin without whom it had been foretold that the world would fall. The King of the Gods quickly learned that the oracle spoke the truth as his thunderbolts glanced off harmlessly, mere sparks of static; the giants were immune to divine wrath. Gaea searched for a herb to make them immune from Hercules' strength as well, but Zeus extinguished the moon and the sun and by the light of the stars plucked away this plant before Mother Earth could find it.

Immediately upon Hercules' arrival, he dropped the giants' general Alcyoneus with his bow, but to his astonishment the giant quickly regained his feet, stronger than before. Wise Athena warned him of the prophecy that as long as the monster fought on his native soil he could not be slain. So the son of Zeus picked up the roaring giant and carried him across the border to neighboring Macedonia, and there ended the general's life.

In the hero's absence the giants launched a successful counter-offensive and beat the gods back to the slopes of Olympus. There Porphyrion prepared to ravish the helpless Hera but her namesake, Hercules, returned in the nick of time. Despite all the many injustices Hera had rained down on her stepson throughout his life, Hercules acted without hesitation to protect her and shot her attacker dead with an arrow. From that moment a slow turn began within Hera's breast. From then on, her hatred for Hercules faded until it no longer had any hold on her heart whatsoever.

The death of Porphyrion turned the tide of battle. Apollodorus explains:

> As for the other giants, Ephialtes was shot by Apollo with an arrow in his left eye and by Hercules in his right; Eurytus was killed by Dionysus with a thyrsus [staff], and Clytius by Hecate with torches, and Mimas by Hephaestus with missiles of red-hot metal. Enceladus fled, but Athena threw on him in his flight the island of Sicily; and she flayed Pallas and used his skin to shield her own body in the fight. Polybotes was chased through the sea by Poseidon and came to Cos; and Poseidon, breaking off that piece of the island which is called Nisyrum, threw it on him. And Hermes, wearing the helmet of Hades, slew Hippolytus in the fight, and Artemis slew Gration. And the Fates, fighting with brazer clubs, killed Agrius and Thoas.

The battle raged on until Zeus and Hercules came together and fought side by side. Zeus used his mighty thunderbolts to knock the giants down and then Hercules finished them off with his bow and poisoned arrows. In this way, the father and son destroyed all of the remaining giants.

(Opposite) Hercules rescued Hera from the clutches of the Giants during their uprising against Olympus; as a result their long-time feud was at last put to rest.

Heaven was saved; the prophesy upon the hero's birth was fulfilled; and, perhaps most importantly, Hercules made peace with his lifelong tormentor and looked forward to a life with the shadow of Hera's vengeance no longer cast over him.

Death and Rebirth

Though the reason for his existence had been fulfilled, Hercules had many more adventures, far too many to be mentioned any more than in passing here. With the help of Athena he slew Ares' monstrous son Cycnus, immortalized by Hesiod in his poem *The Shield of Heracles*. Framed by the master thief Autolycus for stealing the horses of Prince Iphitus of Euboea, Hercules murdered the noble youth in an indignant rage after being accused of the crime, and was forced back into slavery as punishment. He was bought by Omphale, Queen of Lydia, and served her for nearly three years, often in women's clothing.

In an archery contest he won the right to marry Iole, Princess of Oechalia, but her father refused to give her to a man who already had a bride. He accused Hercules of having won the contest through magic, and being thus ineligible for the prize. Like many before him, King Eurytus learned the price of angering Hercules. His city was leveled, his treasure looted, he and all his sons were murdered. Horrified by the death of her father and brothers, Iole hurled herself from the castle battlements but her wide skirts billowed out as she fell, slowing her fall and forcing her to land unharmed.

Collecting his human trophy, Hercules sent Iole to Trachis to be installed in Deianira's house. By this point she had been married for many years to the son of Zeus and had borne him many children. Though she was used to his compulsive philandering, being forced to share her home with one of his mistresses was too great an insult to bear. (Sophocles: "I fear that Heracles will soon be called my husband, but this younger woman's man.")

Deianira did not forget what the centaur Nessus had told her about his shirt being an irresistible aphrodisiac. She ordered Hercules' servant Lichas to carry the raiment to her husband while he prepared to sacrifice to his father on the Cenaean headland in celebration of his victory – ostensibly, it was a gift from her to be worn during the ceremony. She left strict instructions that none but Hercules should wear it, and he should put it on only as the dawning sun rose.

Hercules followed these instructions to the letter, and the moment he donned the shirt the world knew the full extent of the centaur's treachery. The tunic was stained with blood that had been poisoned by the gall of the hydra by way of Hercules' arrows, which now poisoned him with unbearable fire as the light of the sun hit it. In an insensate rage he smashed away Lichas, the servant who gave him the shirt. The poor man splattered across the rocks of the cape that still bears his name today.

The hero tried to rip the shirt off him, but it was already seared to his flesh, the poison seeping all the way to the marrow in his bones. The only way to end Hercules' pain was death. The great hero's last words forgave Deianira for falling prey to the centaur's deceptions, for there had been a prophecy from Zeus that "No man alive may ever kill Hercules; a dead enemy shall be his downfall." (Nevertheless, wracked with guilt, she hanged herself.) He then gave Iole to his son Hyllus as his bride and hurled himself on his own funeral pyre.

LA MORT D'HERCULE.
The death of Hercules.

Der Todt von Hercules.
De Doodt van Hercules.

When he next awoke, Hercules found himself in Olympus, rejoined with his father and reborn as a new god. He was asked to join The Twelve Olympians who were held in the greatest esteem by the Greek people. The hosts of Heaven applauded as Hercules, reconciled with his stepmother, emerged from beneath Hera's skirts in a symbolic rebirth, now as the Goddess of Marriage's true son. To seal their peace for all time, Hera offered her own daughter Hebe, Goddess of Youth, as Hercules' heavenly wife.

And here, with the eternity of godhood, does the story of Hercules end. The savior of man and gods had performed his final labor, and though brought low by the one who loved him most, he was rewarded with immortality. We shall leave it to the reader to decide his or her own answer to the question the American poet Richmond Lattimore had him ask, in his moments of doubt, if he had chosen rightly at that long-ago crossroads:

Was it worth
The beating it took to pacify and set right a world torn inside out,
And fight his way to being the best man on earth?

(Overleaf) Hercules's divine father, Zeus, welcomes the hero to sit among the Twelve Olympians after his death and apotheosis.

73

ON TELEVISION

On the small screen, Hercules has scored a couple of successes. To capitalize on the cinematic success of the sword-and-sandal genre, Trans-Lux Television Enterprises, who brought Felix the Cat to the small screen, syndicated the kids' cartoon *Mighty Hercules* from 1964 to 1966. Herc descends from Mount Olympus to fight evil, but has to wear a magic ring (with a giant "H" on it, of course) to avoid losing his godly powers on the mortal plane. He battles bizarrely warped mythological mash-ups of wizards, monsters, and sea beasts, though many viewers would have cheered if he had given his centaur sidekick Newton a smack too, for he had the annoying habit of saying all his lines twice.

Three decades later the son of Zeus returned to syndicated TV, this time in the form of actor Kevin Sorbo. The Sam Raimi-produced *Hercules: The Legendary Journeys* was an hour-long adventure that ran from 1995 to 1999 across 111 episodes. Another hodgepodge of mythological elements, Hercules and his (apparently totally platonic) companion Iolaus adventure across the ancient world through a mélange of time periods and cultural influences, often evading the schemes of wrathful Hera. It is a rare show that is best known for a more successful spinoff, in this case, *Xena: Warrior Princess*, which outlasted its antecedent by two years.

Kevin Sorbo in action in *Hercules: The Legendary Journeys*. (Corbis)

HERCULES THE GOD

Pedants insist on referring to Hercules as a "demigod" due to his half-human heritage. Plutarch sniffs that he "was not a legitimate god, but had something alien about him, from the fact that his mother was a mortal." One would think that after dying and ascending to Heaven he would be recognized with full divine status, but this was apparently in dispute even in ancient times. Pausanias describes the conflict that inspired the annual Herculean festival in southern Greece:

> The story is that on coming to the Sikyonian land Phaistos found the people giving offerings to Heracles as to a hero. Phaistos then refused to do anything of the kind, but insisted on sacrificing to him as a god. Even at the present day the Sikyonians, after slaying a lamb and burning the thighs upon the altar, eat some of the meat as part of a victim given to a god, while the rest they offer as to a hero. The first day of the festival in honor of Heracles they name [text missing]; the second they call Heracleia.

Athena herself drives the chariot that carries Hercules to Olympus after his death. (Mary Evans)

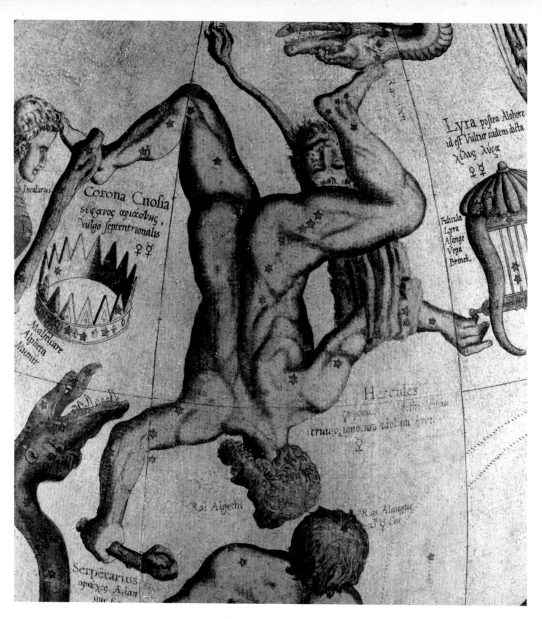

Hercules and Corona Borealis constellations from the Mercator celestial globe from a sixteenth-century map. (PD-US)

Pausanias rattles off a number of altars to Heracles, and many to his wife, Hebe, inside the city limits of Athens alone. Citizens would hold a festival, the Heracleia, annually upon the hero's death. In Thebes, his hometown, the festival lasted days at a time. The people of Marathon boasted that they were the first to regard the hero as a god, and claimed that he, along with Theseus, gave them divine assistance in their legendary victory in the Persian War in 490 BCE. In Elis, birthplace of the Olympics, Hercules' shrines would be found in gymnasiums where competitors would dedicate prayers and sacrifices before matches. In Nemea there was even a tomb for the finger he was said to have lost fighting its invincible lion.

Beyond Greece, Hercules was worshipped throughout the Mediterranean world. He was called upon to slay the "daemons" of plague in Ionia (Turkey). An island named after him in the Black Sea was considered entirely sacred to the hero god, and not even its wild grapes could be picked without fear of offending him.

Cicero, commenting from Rome, classifies Heracles as one of "a number of deified human beings" that the Greeks worshipped. To the statesman's dismay, Julius Caesar himself would soon be treated as a god along with his successors (his right-hand man, Marc Antony, claimed direct descent from Hercules), and the Imperials quickly adopted the worship of Hercules as a divine reflection of the strength they hoped to project upon the world. On returning to the Imperial capital after victory in battle, Roman generals would pay their respects to the robed statue of the son of Zeus at the small domed chapel Hercules Triumphalis between the Tiber and the Circus Maximus. At Hercules' stone feet a tenth of the general's loot would be laid, to be distributed to the people after a triumphal procession. Another temple, Great Altar of Unconquered Hercules (Herculis Invicti Ara Maxima), this with a bronze statue, stood by the Porta Trigemina until the Catholic Church had it torn down in the fifteenth century. It had been built at the spot where Hercules was said to sacrifice to his father Zeus after his defeat of Cacus during the Tenth Labor. The Romans spread their love of Hercules far and wide; generals erected altars to Hercules in their conquered lands of Spain and France. Archeologists discovered a temple to the son of Zeus in Egypt's Bahariya Oasis in 1996. The mere fact that he is known better now by his adopted Roman name than his given Greek one is testament in itself to his popularity throughout the Empire.

Judging by his widespread worship, it seems the question of Hercules' godhood was answered decidedly in his favor.

GLOSSARY

Aberration: Something that deviates from the norm.

Amphora: An ancient Greek vase that is oval-shaped with a narrow neck and two handles.

Aphrodisiac: An agent that causes sexual desire.

Cataclysm: A sudden large-scale event marked by violence and upheaval.

Centaur: A mythical creature combining the body of a horse with the torso of a human.

Epitome: A perfect representation.

Eromenos: A young man who has a sexual relationship with an older man; the plural is *eromenoi*.

Flag: To drop in energy or interest.

Grotto: A small cave, or a recess made in the earth to resemble a cave.

Hind: A female red deer.

Hydra: A mythical creature with many heads that regenerate when one is slayed.

Impetuous: Impulsive; done quickly and without thought or care.

Outré: Unconventional or unusual.

Pankration: A combat sport invented in ancient Greece that resembles modern-day mixed martial arts; from the Greek for "all" ("pan") and "strength" ("kratos").

Penitence: Regret for having done wrong.

Pyre: A pile of combustible material for burning a body in a funeral rite.

Scourge: A person or thing that causes a lot of trouble or suffering.

Temerity: Recklessness; the quality of being unafraid of danger.

Tyrant: A ruler who has absolute power and oppresses those under his or her control.

Usurper: Someone who takes power illegally.

FOR MORE INFORMATION

The American Classical League
Miami University
422 Wells Mill Drive
Oxford, OH 45056
(513) 529-7741
Website: http://www.aclclassics.org
The American Classical League fosters the study of classical languages in the
    United States and Canada by offering teaching resources, sponsoring
    workshops and summer institutes, and publishing newsletters.

The British Museum
Department of Greece and Rome
Great Russell Street
London WC1B 3DG
England
+44 (0)20 7323 8321
Website: http://www.britishmuseum.org/about_us/departments/greece_
    and_rome.aspx
The British Museum boasts one of the largest, most comprehensive
    collections of antiquities from ancient Greece and Rome. Among its
    most notable sculptures are remnants of the Parthenon in Athens, the
    Mausoleum at Halikarnassos, and the Temple of Artemis at Ephesos.

The Classical Association of Canada
Université Laval
Département d'histoire 1030
av. des Sciences-Humaines
Québec, QC G1V 0A6
Canada
Website: http://cac-scec.ca/wordpress/index/
The Classical Association of Canada advances the study of the Greek and
    Roman civilizations and their later influence on modern culture,
    encouraging the teaching of classical languages and civilizations in
    Canadian education at all levels.

The Society for Classical Studies
University of Pennsylvania
220 S. 40th Street, Suite 201E
Philadelphia, PA 19104-3512

(215) 898-4975
Website: http://www.apaclassics.org
Originally founded in 1869 as the American Philological Association, the
    Society for Classical Studies promotes the study of ancient Greek and
    Roman languages, literatures, and civilizations. It produces scholarly
    journals, fosters wider public appreciation of the classics, and
    coordinates activities for teaching the classics to students of all ages.

The Stavros Niarchos Foundation Centre for Hellenic Studies
Simon Fraser University
8888 University Drive
Burnaby, BC V5A 1S6
Canada
Website: http://www.sfu.ca/snfchs.html
This center supports the teaching of Greek history, language, and culture
    through teaching and research. Via its New Media Lab, the center
    offers online tutoring in Greek, a guide to the city of Athens, and
    other e-learning projects.

University of Pennsylvania Museum of Archaeology and Anthropology
3260 South Street
Philadelphia, PA 19104
(215) 898-4000
Website: http://www.penn.museum
The Greece Gallery at this museum reveals the daily life, religion, commerce
    and trade, and burial practices of ancient Greek society. Its collection
    features thousands of artifacts dating from 3000 BCE to the fifth
    century CE, some of which can be viewed on its website.

WEBSITES

Because of the changing nature of Internet links, Rosen Publishing has
developed an online list of websites related to the subject of this book. This
site is updated regularly. Please use this link to access this list:

http://www.rosenlinks.com/HERO/Herc

FOR FURTHER READING

Bryant, Megan E. *Oh My Gods! A Look-It-Up Guide to the Gods of Mythology* (Mythlopedia). New York, NY: Scholastic, 2010.

Bulfinch, Thomas. *Bulfinch's Mythology*. CreateSpace, 2010.

Day, Malcolm. *100 Characters from Classical Mythology: Discover the Fascinating Stories of the Greek and Roman Deities*. Hauppauge, NY: Barron's Educational Series, 2007.

Dell, Christopher. *Mythology: The Complete Guide to Our Imagined Worlds*. London, England: Thames & Hudson, 2012.

Ehrmann, Johanna. *The Labors of Heracles* (Jr. Graphic Myths: Greek Myths). New York, NY: Powerkids Press, 2014.

Euripides. "Alcestis" and "The Children of Heracles." In *Euripides* I, 3rd ed., edited by David Grene, Richmond Lattimore, Mark Griffith, and Glenn W. Most. Chicago, IL: The University of Chicago Press, 2013.

Euripides. *Grief Lessons: Four Plays by Euripides*. Trans. Anne Carson. New York, NY: New York Review Books, 2006.

Evans, Lady Hestia. *Mythology: The Gods, Heroes, and Monsters of Ancient Greece*. Somerville, MA: Candlewick Press, 2007.

Hamby, Zachary. *Greek Mythology for Teens: Classic Myths in Today's World*. Waco, TX: Prufrock Press, 2011.

Hamilton, Edith. *Mythology: Timeless Tales of Gods and Heroes*. Reprint edition. New York, NY: Grand Central Publishing, 2011.

Impelluso, Lucia. *Myths: Tales of the Greek and Roman Gods*. New York, NY: Abrams, 2008.

Jeffrey, Gary. *Hercules Fights the Nemean Lion* (Graphic Mythical Heroes). New York, NY: Gareth Stevens Publishing, 2013.

Napoli, Donna Jo. *Treasury of Greek Mythology: Classic Stories of Gods, Goddesses, Heroes & Monsters*. Des Moines, IA: National Geographic Children's Books, 2011.

Ovid. *Metamorphoses*. Trans. A.D. Melville. Reissue edition. Oxford, England: Oxford University Press, 2008.

Pak, Greg, and Fred Van Lente. *The Incredible Hercules: Against the World*. New York, NY: Marvel Comics, 2008.

Riordan, Rick. *The Lost Hero* (Heroes of Olympus). New York, NY: Disney-Hyperion, 2010.

Riordan, Rick. *Percy Jackson and the Olympians* (Paperback Boxed Set). New York, NY: Disney-Hyperion, 2014.

Taft, Michael, ed. *Greek Gods and Goddesses* (Gods and Goddesses of Mythology). New York, NY: Britannica Educational Services, 2014.

Index